Just Like That

Sharon Gilman

First Printing: January 2019

ISBN- 9781793948144

Edited by Susan Van Gulick
Cover & interior design by Amy Allen Designs

Contents

This book is dedicated to my wonderful husband
who has been full of wisdom and support throughout
the writing of this book. And what a "green thumb"
groundskeeper he continues to be!

Prologue

The apostle John said in John 20:30 *"Many other signs Jesus also performed, which are not written in this book; but these have been written so that you may believe that Jesus is the Christ, the Son of God and that believing you may have life in His name."*

So I add my testimony to the voice of John in the pages of this book that I write. These things that I write have been written so that through my testimony you may believe that Jesus is the Christ, the Son of God and that believing you may have life in His name.

I'm certain every child of God will be called upon to bear witness of God's Gracious, Active Presence in their lives. This is the witness I bear, and I'm compelled to share it and join the throngs of others who have experienced undeniably the Loving Hand of God.

John ends his gospel saying, *"There are also many things which Jesus did, which if they were written in detail, I suppose that even the world itself would not contain the books that would be written."*

Beginnings

It was a cold, dark, early morning, except for a light dusting of snow that had fallen during the night, giving the Detroit city streets and sidewalks a diamond-like sparkle. The fading intensity of the street lights above were illuminating one last beautiful glimmer in the snow before dawn completely outshone with day. My father had risen earlier and parked the car as close to the doorway of our terrace as possible. He helped my mother as she attempted to walk through the snow to the car. Approaching the car, my father lifted my mother and sat her ever so gently in the seat. Their early departure this morning and his special care was reflective of her condition. She was going into labor! They had been married 10 years and I was their first and only child, Sharon Marie Siler born in Detroit, Michigan on November 19, 1942.

The tenderness with which my father responded to my mother on that cold November morning is the same tenderness she and I received from him throughout my life. He was a strong man who lived by principle; honest, kind and good. His positive influence on my life is something I have cherished. I remember as a teenager asking him what made him so good. I gave him a list of all his virtues. He looked me in the eye with great intensity and said, "Oh honey, all my righteousness is as filthy rags." At the time I didn't know that response was taken from the pages of the Bible and held with it a deep profound truth for us all.

My early childhood was spent in the hustle and bustle of the city. The bus stop, directly in front of our little brick terrace (8817 Third Street) was the bus stop pick-up point to take people deeper into the inner city. Every time the big city bus pulled away it left with a loud roar and a large puff of gases (this happened every 20 minutes). The tall, towering buildings of the city obscured the horizon so that the beauty of the sunrise and the sunset was never visible. The horizon was completely covered with dark skyscrapers and the bright, red ball on the Fisher Building was the only thing my eye caught as I gazed into the night. My only exposure to a sunrise or sunset or a sky filled with stars was through pictures. I believed sunsets and stars only happened in the days of my grandparents, who lived in the back roads of Kentucky where time stood still, and those beautiful things still existed. Nonetheless, within this environment, I was loved and cared for.

My parents established a Christian home with morals and integrity. However, I don't remember either of them reading the Bible in front of me or encouraging me to know what it said. In those early years, church was a part of our lives as a family. On one occasion, I recall being seated in a pew between my parents. I was so little and young that my legs didn't bend over the wooden pew but extended out stiffly in front of me. My white shoes, having been polished that morning for the occasion, were

everything I could see, until I glanced up to see my father.

His eyes were closed, and his head was bowed. I turned and asked Momma what was wrong with Daddy. She quietly said, "Daddy is praying." As little as I was, I knew that this was something important and I have remembered that sight in my mind all these years. Also, even though I have no actual recollection of the time, I have a photo of myself in the 3-year old's graduating class. Life was wonderful, and my momma and daddy were everything to me.

When I turned school age, I was sent to the public school, Crossman Elementary, that was within walking distance from our terrace. The school was racially mixed so as I got into the first and second grade, and because I was blonde with blue eyes and only one of seven white children in the class of 26 or so, I had difficulty fitting in. As a result, I was bullied. On one occasion, I was chased home by two boys, one with a knife. At other times, I remember physically defending myself with both boys and girls and sometimes, on my walk home, I was taunted. These things didn't shock me, and I was never seriously hurt. I never shared with my parents any of these episodes. I believed that this was normal; just the way things were in school.

However, because I always seemed to be in the middle of trouble, I was sent to the principal's office. The principal told me that because lunch time and recess seemed to be the worst time for me, I had lost my privilege to eat lunch at school. I certainly didn't want to tell my parents how bad I was and that I had lost my privilege to eat at school! So I continued to bring my lunch. A sweet little black girl told me that I could go home with her and eat with her and that I would not need to tell my mother. That sounded like a good plan to me. Each day I went home with her. There was never anyone at home. We ate in peace, and everything seemed to be working out until one day the principal noticed that I had my lunch with me. She asked me, "Why did you bring your lunch with you, when I told you that you had lost your privilege to eat at school?" The only answer I could give her was, "My mother wants me to." Well, the next thing I knew, the principal called my parents and I was taken out of school!

A New Home

My mother had made arrangements for me to go live with my mother's sister, Aunt Ree and her husband, Uncle Andrew and my 10-year-old cousin, Judy. They lived in Detroit also but they were on the outskirts, away from the inner city and living now in a different neighborhood, so I could attend school with Judy. Hopefully this would give me a chance to start fresh in a new school. Aunt Ree, short for Marie, (I was named after her) and Uncle Andrew were good, kind and honest people. Everyone thought that Judy, being three years older than I and an only child also, may find my presence enjoyable.

I didn't realize it at the time, but this decision was not solely based on the difficulty I was having in school. My mother had been told by the doctors that she had a large tumor. Now my mother had one flaw. She was very fearful! She wouldn't ride across a bridge in a car! My dad would have to let her out to walk across it. Then he would drive across. She used stairs instead of the elevator! She was afraid of water and would never go swimming! She wouldn't fly in an airplane! If she had a pain, she always took it to be something fatal. The list goes on. My father was a kind, gentle, man who loved my mother with a deep devotion. I believe that when he married her, being six years older than she, he keenly felt a duty to treat her with a special kindness. He knew of her fears before they were married, and he never wanted to demand anything of her that would scare her or cause her to lose trust in him. So, we lived with these things...but it was just a part of my mother and we loved her. She never imposed her fears on me, however when the arrangement was made for me to live with my Aunt Ree, this diagnosis of the tumor was on her mind. She believed that she probably would die and leave me without a mother, so she wanted to make sure that I was cared for during her surgery and if need be, if she died, in the care of her sister to raise me. So, at this point, 7 years old, I found myself living with Judy and her family...in my new home.

Judy

Being three years older than I was, Judy was very influential in my life. I wanted to do everything she could do. She took piano lessons once a week and could play beautifully. She was playing difficult, classical pieces and everything she mastered, I wanted to play. Sometimes in the summer when the windows and doors were opened and while Judy was practicing the piano, the neighborhood kids would stop in front of the house just to listen to her practice. Judy was also very artistic. She could draw anything, and her art work was beautiful! She was creative! She created a pretend grocery store down in her basement, filling the shelves with the empty cans and boxes that Aunt Ree had opened upside down so that when we put them on the shelves they looked full and unopened. She had a toy cash register and a checkout counter, and our imaginations did the rest. When she received miniature plastic cowboys and horses (I loved horses) for a Christmas gift, she also created a miniature ranch for them in which she added fencing, a bunk house, a clothes line hanging small cut out forms of shirts and pants, with tiny broken toothpicks for clothes pins. Judy provided endless things to do.

There was not much said about Jesus in Aunt Ree's home but there was always the sense of God's reality and Jesus' importance. They always expected Judy and me to say our prayers at night, and the blessing before each dinner meal: "We fold our hands, we bow our heads, we thank You Lord for this good bread. We thank You for the world so sweet. We thank You for the food we eat. We thank You for the birds that sing. We thank You God for everything."

Judy and I would say this prayer in unison every evening meal. Because WWII had ended, and I was very much aware of the war that had been won, I always said at the end of the prayer, "And let there be peace on earth all along. In Jesus' Name, Amen."

In 1945, when I was 3 years old the smiling, victorious soldiers were coming home from the War in parade style, sitting on the back seats of opened convertibles. 8817 Third Street was directly on the parade route right in front of our terrace. We were all outside on the terrace porch, waving and beating on pots and pans, shouting happily! Everyone was so exuberant that there was peace! I was very impressed. No one ever commented on my addition to the prayer or made me feel awkward. And now I know in a fallen world this time of peace on earth all along will come but not until God's Perfect Timing.

Uncle Andrew was often seen reading his Bible. Aunt Ree told me that Uncle Andrew had never said a curse word in his life nor had he ever had a drink of alcohol. When I heard that, it made me want to do the same thing and I purposed in my heart to do just that. But I don't remember ever going to church when I lived with them. Judy also shared her room with me, including her dresser and closet and her full-sized bed. She would, however, get pretty upset when I would get on her side of the bed. One day she took her finger and drew an imaginary line down the middle of the bed saying, "See this line? If you get over this line, I'm going to pound that part of your body!" It didn't take long, with a few poundings, and I learned never to get any part of my body on her side of the bed!

I began to have trouble sleeping at night and would get very frightened. If I could go to sleep before Judy went to sleep I would be fine, but if she went to sleep first I would be so frightened that I would wake up Aunt Ree, calling for her. She was not very sympathetic with my problem and would just sternly tell me to go to sleep. One time, Judy was invited to an overnight and I would have to sleep by myself. This was terrifying to me! I dreaded it when that night finally came. As usual, fear set in. Judy was not there! Aunt Ree was not there for me! I was so frightened that I could not move! My arms were held straight down on my sides. I was lying on my back...frozen. I couldn't have been feeling more threatened or vulnerable. At that point, I remembered Jesus! My introduction to Jesus was very scant, but I remembered that He was Kind.

Church and Jesus were not discussed much in my childhood experiences. Even though my family would call themselves Christians, I don't remember much emphasis on the Word of God or conversations that would have addressed situations like this. As I think about this now, I'm reminded of the stronghold that fear had on my mother's life. But in my situation here, I remembered Jesus! So there, in my fear and the darkness of the night, I asked Jesus to hold my hand and be with me. As I lay there, I felt a gentle light touch envelop the back of my right hand and encase it. I closed my eyes, my body relaxed, and I didn't feel anything else until it was morning! In surprise, I raised up and looked over on Judy's side of the bed, expecting to see a bed untouched. Instead, the pillow was crushed right in the center with a circle indention! The indentation from the pillow, on the top blanket, extended down to the foot of the bed. I was so thrilled! I had gotten through my greatest fear and Jesus did it! This was the first experience of my life where I had witnessed the reality of God in my personal need...it was only the beginning!

As time went on, I began to miss Momma and Daddy more and more. There were long stretches of time when I didn't see them. When they would come, sometimes after a visit, the cry for them after they left was so deep I felt sick. Once my mother left her purse. I clung to that purse like it was her and sobbed like there was no hope in ever seeing her again. On occasion, I spent the weekend with them and on Monday morning Daddy would drive me to the school. I remember turning and looking at him sitting behind the steering wheel, as I walked up to the school door. He sat there still, staring at me. When I got out of his sight, the tears would flow again, and I would start my day of school upset and could think of nothing else but being with them. My teacher asked me why I was crying. I told her that I could only see my parents on the weekends and that I missed them when I had to say goodbye. I feel certain that this was shared with my family, however no one ever told me that the teacher ever said anything.

While I lived with Aunt Ree, and after my mother's surgery, my parents took a trip to California. They visited one of my mother's other sisters, Aunt Jo. My mother had four sisters. I believe that this was part of my mother's healing. Aunt Jo was level-headed, and her thinking probably convinced my mother that she was not going to die. They were gone many weeks, but when they returned, my daddy burst through the front door of Aunt Ree's house, grabbed me with hugs that nearly smothered me, saying with deep emotion, "We will never leave you again!" And they never did.

8817 Third Street, Here I Come!

I was able to move back with my parents and I couldn't have been happier! But there was one big change. After talking to the teachers and principal it was determined that to return to the situation at Crossman Elementary would be a mistake. There were alternatives. Would my parents consider a private school? I really don't know how they managed to afford the tuition and I know they must have sacrificed. For one school year I was enrolled at Miss Newman's, an all-girls school, not too far from our terrace. I was in a classroom of seven girls, my age and grade. The private school bus would stop every morning at the bus stop in front of our terrace and I would join my classmates on the ride to school. That year was wonderful. I enjoyed the girls and developed friendships. The teacher had time to give to each of us but best of all I was with my momma and daddy and there were no more tears. I was nine years old.

During this time, on occasion we attended a Baptist church and most of all I remember Sunday School. Our teacher challenged us to memorize John 14:1:

"Let not your heart be troubled; you believe in God believe also in Me. In my Father's house are many mansions. If it were not so I would have told you. I go to prepare a place for you. And if I go to prepare a place for you, I will come again and receive you to Myself that where I am, there you may be also."

Those who memorized this were given a Bible bookmark. The bookmark was unusual to me, in that it was all cloth and the words of the Psalm 23 were embroidered on it. It was lovely, so I worked very hard to memorize the passage. That was the first Scripture I ever memorized, and it has stayed with me until this very day. I kept the bookmark many years. Our teacher also spoke of Heaven and told us about the new bodies that the Lord was going to give us. She pointed to the large thick veins in her hands saying that those would not be there and that our skin would be smooth and beautiful. I listened intently and believed everything she said.

My mother was always looking for ways to make me comfortable before an audience so for the opening exercise of the Sunday School, my mother asked the superintendent if I could play the piano. When I was called up to play, I played "Jesus Loves Me" without any mistakes but I forgot to take my little dress gloves off so, I played the entire piece with gloves on! I really did enjoy Sunday School, but I didn't know that soon I would be leaving Miss Newman's, this church and 8817 Third Street.

Kentucky

Kentucky was where my parents were born and where we visited each summer. It was filled with rolling hills, green pastures, grazing cows and horses, chickens, fresh eggs, fresh vegetables from the garden and most appreciated, a wonderful grandma and grandpa we called, "Mamaw" and "Papaw." They gave birth to eight children (five girls and three boys) and most of them stayed in Kentucky. As a result we had lots of cousins.

Our summer visits included Judy because she and Aunt Ree would join us for the road trip. Uncle Andrew would come too, if he could get time off from work. Upon arrival, we were provided many days of childhood activity with two of our favorite cousins, Frank and Libby. They were closest to our ages, and I was the youngest. Aunt Jenny was their mother and she and Uncle Ed welcomed Judy and me as their own. The rolling hills and hallows were a great place to play. My cousins and I loved to swing on a great vine that hung from a large tree over one of the hallows on the mountainside. As we would swing we would squeal and gasp, feeling the vine drop slightly from its place, and each of us would dare the other to try again.

Sometimes Mamaw and Papaw's dusty road was still traveled by wagons drawn by mules or horses. As we heard the rattling, rolling wheels coming, one of us would shout, "Let's hop the wagon!" Running as fast as we could behind the slowly moving, old, weather-worn wagon, we would jump up and ride on the back; bouncing and jostling until we came to Mamaw and Papaw's seven-bedroom farm house right along the road. We would sit on their big porch swing at night taking turns telling scary stories. The lightening bugs were fun too. We would try to catch them and put them in a jar.

One afternoon, Judy, Libby, Frank and I went exploring down in Mamaw's cellar. There were steps leading down to a low ceiling area. It was dark and damp and had a dirt floor. It was intriguing and just calling for kids to investigate. Judy was the one who thought about going on these adventures. She was so creative and always thought of doing things no one else would ever dream. When we went down the dark steps the light from the living area upstairs illuminated the steps, so we just kept following the lighted steps. Soon we saw all the things that were piled and discarded - too good to keep but not useful anymore. There were old tables, boxes piled with books, old containers, empty paint cans, a rocking chair, among many other things too lengthy to mention, but in particular, an old spinning wheel. One paint can was heavy with paint and the lid could be pried open! To our pleasant surprise the paint was useable, and old paint brushes were handy. The color of the paint was barn red. We painted everything! I particularly remember painting the old spinning wheel! Our Mamaw or Papaw never expressed any displeasure in what we had done, nor did our parents. They may not even have known what we did; the cellar being a place infrequently visited. Those days spent with them were the highlight of my life! I looked forward to every summer "going to Kentucky!"

Aunt Kathleen

When my father became an adult and married my mother (they were neighbors from birth), Kentucky was not the place to find a good paying job. He had been educated as a teacher and school administrator, and had held positions in schools; however, the income was not enough to support a family. That precipitated their decision to move to Detroit before I was born. He worked in Ypsilanti on an assembly line for the Ford Motor Company. My parents were frugal, renting the terrace in the inner city for $50 per month. There were three bedrooms upstairs and they rented those out, one for $10 and the other two for $7 each per week. They converted the dining room, with closed doors for privacy, into a bedroom which I shared with them. Because of this arrangement, the rental of the rooms upstairs covered their housing expense with plenty left over. They were able to get ahead and pursue other options for employment.

They had heard that in Lexington, Kentucky, where another one of my mother's five sisters and her family lived, there were job opportunities. This sister, my Aunt Kathleen, was the first one in the family that I had ever heard talk about Jesus often and openly. She saw Jesus in everything! She and her family went to a large church in Lexington, and she tried to persuade my mother and father to attend regularly too. We never did. I remember one particular incident, when on a Sunday afternoon, we were visiting them. Their hand-push mower was setting in the backyard. I asked Aunt Kathleen if I could mow their backyard. I was 10 years old and the task was way too big for a 10-year-old…but that was not Aunt Kathleen's focus. She said, "Oh, this is the day of worship. We don't work on Sunday. Today is our day of rest. Mowing the lawn would be work." I asked, "Even if I would think it would be fun?" She said, "Oh yes, even if you think it would be fun. The day is set aside for God." I never forgot her steadfast conviction. The impact Aunt Kathleen had on me during that one year in Lexington was lasting. I saw a life fully committed to God and bold enough to talk about it.

It seemed to my parents that Detroit was still the best place to find a job that could support our family, so we returned to Detroit after a year. We rented a flat close to Aunt Ree and Uncle Andrew. It was fun to see Judy again, but because she was now 14 and I was almost 12, there seemed to be a big difference in our ages; she was a teenager and I was still in the world of a child. She was involved with her life and I was involved in mine. So we didn't see one another often.

Soon after we had returned to Detroit, we received a long-distance phone call. I heard my mother talking. It was Aunt Kathleen…she shared the terrible news that she had been diagnosed with cancer. In those days, cancer meant sure death. At that point, the doctors were doing all they could, but a year later, she passed away leaving her husband and their 2 young sons. She was only 39 years old. All the family was shocked and deeply grieved, but we all knew that she had left a sure and powerful testimony of Christ and His promises of Eternal Life. Even her last months of life here on earth were filled with her unfailing conviction in God's Love and care for her. Her last hours were filled with visions of heaven, angels, people and all that awaited her. She was the first I had ever seen in a casket. Huge and abundant baskets of flowers surrounded her, and the fragrance of the flowers filled the area…just like the fragrance of her life. All knew she was with the Lord…and so did I.

Martha, The Song Bird

It was Fall of 1954. I was 12 years old and Tappan Junior High in Detroit was to be my new school. In September I would be in this brand-new school with brand-new schoolmates and teachers. This large city school accommodated several thousand students. It was massive and beautifully constructed in brick with colorful tiles over the entry doors. Judy's high school was even more impressive. Uncle Andrew, after seeing these city schools, remarked, "They sure beat the one room school house I attended as a boy in Mississippi!"

All new students were to meet in the auditorium for registration. Parents or guardians were to accompany their students to register them. There were hundreds of students and parents there. The air was electric with excitement. My mother knew that the newness of everything might be overwhelming for me so she (behind the scenes) got acquainted with a mom and her daughter that seemed to be a good fit for friendship. She discovered that the mom had the same concerns that she had. She too, had been looking for a good friend for her daughter. Martha was her daughter's name and our friendship became more important than any of us knew at the time.

We continued our friendship outside of school, even though we were inseparable at school. We always waited for each other so that we would walk together to each class. Martha could sing beautifully, and she had joined a select group called the "Tappanairs." Tryouts were required before being selected, and of course, Martha had no trouble being included in the group. She encouraged me to try out. I thought there would be no way that I would be selected, even though I had been given piano lessons. (Judy's influence in my time living with them). My mother singing alto and my daddy singing bass would encourage me to sing the soprano part with them. We would often do this in the car. It was fun! They wanted me to be comfortable in singing and playing the piano. To my surprise and their gladness, I was included with this group of 20 as a Tappanair!

Many happy hours were spent singing with this group. Martha was always the soloist placed as the star on the gigantic Christmas tree for the Christmas program presented to the parents. She sang the obbligato part in "Silent Night" which rang out above all the other voices. She was dressed like an angel, with a star on a golden crown, and all the branches of the tree below her were covered with the many singers from the music classes. Lights twinkled on each branch but Martha, the angel with the starry crown on the top, glowed with a brilliance surpassing all. The tree filled the entire height of the stage. It was impressive and so beautiful! All the teachers liked Martha. But Martha took all the attention in stride. She was my best friend and I was so proud of her. She carried her Bible to school each day, and I knew she went to church regularly. I'm sure she sang solos during the worship times, and church was a big part of her life... but one day, she said to me, "You are not a Christian."

I was stunned and defensive. "Yes, I am!" I exclaimed. Nothing was said about this again. I never asked her why or what she thought I should do about it. Time went on and our friendship never changed or dwindled. She taught me how to build on what I had learned during my piano lessons; how to add arpeggios and play the piano by adding notes, runs and cords...and how to sing with confidence.

One day Martha invited me to come to her church. She said that an evangelist was coming and she wondered if I would like to come.

I said, "Sure" remembering what she had stated about me not being a Christian. "I'm a Christian," I thought. "Of course, I'll go." The church was the First Church of the Nazarene. The church was big and full of people. There was excitement and anticipation in the air, but the most important thing I remember about the entire evening was the message brought by the evangelist.

He spoke of Christ's crucifixion in every detail. He spoke of His torture and suffering unimaginable...the beatings and floggings, the nails in His hands and feet, the intense thirst, the weight of His body hanging, producing inexorable pain. The Scriptures he focused on said that He was crushed, pierced, smitten, afflicted...the Lord had caused the iniquity of us all to fall on Him. The chastening for our well-being fell upon Him, and by His scourging we were healed. He was pierced through for our transgressions. He was crushed for our iniquities. I had never heard this before! For the first time I realized what Christ had done for me! For the first time, His crucifixion was personal! It had all gone right to my heart, and I was moved.

Many people went forward to the front of the church, convicted, but I was too embarrassed to let Martha know that, maybe I hadn't been a Christian after all...so I sat in my seat in silence. As we drove home, I forgot about the strong feeling I had. I was just going to move on.

The Calling

The next few days that followed, I had put the experience behind me. Until one day, after school, I walked into my bedroom to change from my school clothes when I heard, a deep voice within myself. I knew it was God's. He said, "I Have Done This For You. WHAT ARE YOU GOING TO DO FOR ME?" I knew to what He was referring. He was referring to His death on the cross for me...He said, "I WANT YOUR LIFE." I said, "Oh no, Lord. You might ask me to do something that I would be scared to do...like go to Africa." (You need to understand, I was only 13 years old). My knowledge of Africa was only through the Abbott and Costello movies I had seen where Abbot was kidnapped by wild Africans with painted faces and bodies. Because they were cannibals, they threw Abbot into a large pot to eat him. Now, when I relate this, it seems very ridiculous to me. But this was my fear and it scared me if the Lord would ask me to be a missionary to Africa. There was no surrender. I couldn't trust God that much!

The next day, I went to school and I didn't think about the conversation with God. But as soon as I went into my bedroom, after school, the Lord spoke to me again. He said, "WHAT ARE YOU GOING TO DO? WILL YOU GIVE ME YOUR LIFE?" Once again, I just couldn't let my fears go. With that response I was left with a deeply felt burden. There was no surrender. But on the third day, I went to school and I didn't think about the conversation with God or my struggle with Him, but as soon as I went into my bedroom, after school, the Lord spoke to me this final time. He said, "WHAT ARE YOU GOING TO DO? WILL YOU GIVE ME YOUR WHOLE LIFE?" At that, I gave my everything to Him! I surrendered it all! I would have my eyes and ears open to follow where He would lead me but for now I would purpose in my heart to go to a Christian college and major in Religion and possiblypursue Christian Education, serving in a church. I wanted Him to guide my life, completely. I felt so free! All that deeply felt burdenwas gone! All the fear was gone! I would even go to Africa! I felt like a ton of bricks had been lifted off my back. I felt so happy! I was excited to see where He would lead! Maybe it would be Africa! At this point in my life, I was 13 years old. My life was all ahead of me and I was giving the whole thing to Him! I trusted Him with everything!

Because Martha had such an unusual talent, her parents decided to send her to a special school, Cass Technical, where she could direct all her studies on voice. I missed her, but I knew her parents were doing the best for her. We did keep in contact for years, but after she married, we lost touch. She married a pastor. She will always be special in my heart. My life took a whole different direction because the Lord had brought her into my life. And I'm grateful to God for giving me a mother who knew the value of Christian friendship

and paved the way for me to be influenced by such a friend.

During this time we had purchased a lovely brick home in Detroit. My mother's family had advised my parents to settle down because, "A rolling stone gathers no moss." We had hopped around from place to place and my parents had come to see that the family's counsel was wise. Our new home was on the outskirts of Detroit on a pretty street lined with

large mature trees that looked like a corridor of green. It was "home" and I began to feel like I had been there all my life.

A very special benefit surfaced very soon after we had moved in. Each day my mother had noticed a young girl, about my age, passing in front of our house, walking her little dachshund. She told me about this girl, saying that it would be nice if I could get acquainted with her. Before long we became very good friends. Eleanor was a cute little blonde with great big blue eyes. She worked in her father's very successful commercial photography business and was able to spend all her earnings on anything she needed, to be probably the most well-dressed, cute, little sophomore at Mackenzie High. I started Mackenzie High as a freshman.

Since I only lived a few houses down the street from her, she said she would give me a ride to school each day. It was a great time to share and talk, so Eleanor being one year older took it upon herself to "teach me the ropes." She was a faithful and good friend. One day she asked me if I wanted to go roller skating at the roller rink with her, her boyfriend, and his friend Harvey. I had met her boyfriend, Therm. He was a nice boy who attended a Baptist Church. I thought it might be fun and I wanted to go. When they came by for me in the car, Eleanor was in the back seat. Harvey was driving and Therm came up to the house to get me. When I approached the car to get in, I thought I would ride with Eleanor, so I jumped in the back seat, not knowing that Eleanor had set up this whole evening as a blind date! I was expected to ride in the front seat with Harvey and skate with him once we got to the roller rink. In my mind, I was going to the roller skating rink to skate, not be a date! I skated all evening, happily alone, paying absolutely no attention to Harvey. I thought he had come to skate too. I had never been on a blind date before. I'm sure Eleanor saw she had a lot more work in "showing me the ropes." I never saw Harvey again and Eleanor never tried to set me up again!

I was now 15 and the commitment I had made to the Lord was still fresh and important to me. My determination never dwindled in the time that had passed since my surrender to Him. My desire was to follow, to the best of my ability, God's leading. As time went by, I began to realize that I needed to be in church. Since Eleanor could drive, I asked her if she would mind driving me to various churches on Sundays to find a church that I could attend. She was happy to do that, but she wasn't interested in attending anywhere regularly. The very first one we went to, was one that my parents had attended years prior, Grand River Avenue Baptist Church. As we went into the sanctuary, I noticed that it wasn't lacking any young people my age and I felt very comfortable there. When my parents heard that I wanted to go to church, and which one I was interested in, they were very encouraging and wholeheartedly agreed to go with me!

The youth group at Grand River Avenue Baptist was alive and active and I was happy to be a part of it and as the new one in the group I was wanting to get involved. On this evening, the youth group leader began talking about an election that needed to be held within our group. The purpose of the election was to select a representative to serve on a committee to plan activities for the youth in our district within the Baptist Convention. The one selected through casting votes, would need to go to regular meetings and represent our church.

All the other districts would be sending representatives also. The voting took place. The one who was chosen by popular vote was Sherry Davis. I didn't know Sherry very well, being so new to the group, but she was beautiful and could sing to match. I was told that often she was asked to sing for the whole church and people were very touched by her talent. She had a sweet delicate voice that seemed to fall from heaven itself...but when the results of the voting reached her ears, she emphatically retorted, "I don't want to go!" The group leader, rather exasperated, threw up his arms asking, "Well, who wants to go?" No one raised their hand. I saw it as an opportunity to serve and follow God's leading, so I raised my hand and said, "I want to go!" I had no idea at that time, that the whole rest of my life rested on those words. This started a chain of events that I never expected.

The first meeting with the district was made up of an adult youth leader and about 10 to 12 young people my age. The leader began explaining the goals of the district, the responsibilities and the expectations. I didn't know anyone in the group, but I felt confident and made it a point to be friendly with the other group members. I was uncommonly talkative, adding my opinion to the discussion, as the group leader continued. Then, when that portion of the leader's presentation was completed, he informed us that we needed to elect a representative from the district to serve on the City Council. The responsibility of the City Council was to plan activities for the Baptist youth of Detroit. When the vote was taken, to my surprise, the group elected me! This was all very strange to me. Why had I been so unusually confident? God's Hand was moving in my young life and someday I would be able to see how He Lovingly directed my steps. Now, instead of the District, I would be serving on the City Council.

It would meet once a month also and I was anxious for the first meeting...it finally came! The group of 10 to 12 was filled with bright, friendly enthusiastic youth. Some of them, I learned, were called, "PKs" or " Preacher's Kids." They were bubbling over with great ideas, for the often 500 participating Baptist youth of Detroit! We would plan gatherings held in some of the larger Baptist churches with special speakers with themes like, *Building Bridges of Brotherly Love*. As members of the council, we would fill in the program with leading in prayer and singing, reading of Scripture, and thought provoking, theme related presentations. The rafters would ring as we sang the familiar hymns and choruses.

We also planned retreats at Camp La Pier, a beautiful Christian Camp where we could organize swimming, boating, fun games and activities and skits with silly costumes and all, and where we laughed so hard our sides hurt. We had special speakers that challenged us to godly living and making Christ Lord of our lives and missionaries that modeled for us lives totally surrendered. The camp fires on the final night of camp were often times of quiet reflection. The silence of the night, except for the crackle of the fire, and the sparks that rose until out of sight, drew us upward to thoughts that could only be led by God; the silence broken as we all sang together, "Give of your best to the Master. Give of the strength of your youth." The dark sky, bursting with the brilliance of the stars of the heavens, seemed to sing, "Amen." So, let it be.

Jim Gilman, Jim Gilman!

While serving on the City Council, any time there was an isolated group of girls together, this person and name would become the conversation. And with good reason! Jim Gilman was the president of our City Council. He was the one who conducted all the monthly City Council meetings. He was the youth chosen to serve in this capacity by the pastor responsible for the council and he seemed to always have the attention of pastors. They mentored and advised him. He was 18 years old and studying to become an industrial engineer, receiving his education through General Motors Institute. With this program, he would be in school for six weeks and work at General Motors for six weeks on a five-year program. This arrangement afforded him the opportunity to serve on the City Council. He was kind to everyone. No one ever heard unkind or crude remarks from him. He led the group with maturity. He was not flirtatious and was never seen with a girl "hanging on his arm." He was very poised as he led those large gatherings of 500 youth. And, he was very, very handsome! But Jim Gilman was very intimidating to me. I had just turned 15 and he seemed bigger than life! I couldn't look at him straight on. When he would say something to me, I had trouble thinking of what to say in return. When the other girls talked about him, I never added anything to the conversation. I only listened.

All these things were going on during my last two years at Mackenzie High. City Council had provided rich opportunities to experience leadership and rich friendships. Grand River Avenue Baptist Church had taught me the discipline and joy of attending church regularly and an added blessing, my parents had been regularly coming with me for both years.

During my Junior and Senior years at Mackenzie, my focus was on the academics. I wanted to have a good grade point average so that I would be accepted in any college. As I worked and studied, I began to look forward to going away to school and all that experience would bring. I was looking forward to majoring in religion, meeting new people and seeing where God was going to lead me. When I expressed these things to my mother, she paused with a slow stare. Then she asked me what I thought about going to Cumberland College. Now Cumberland College was a small Christian college in Williamsburg, Kentucky where Mamaw and Papaw lived and all my extended family. It was a small little town, and everyone knew everyone. At least that is what I thought. It was where I so joyfully visited when I was a child. But at first, it was a disappointment. I guess I was expecting something new and adventurous; something I had never seen before. But I knew my parents had sacrificed many times for me, so I wanted to comply. Cumberland it would be!

Summer was coming to an end. The golden rod in Michigan was tall and in full bloom, a sure sign that autumn was around the corner. But more importantly, their bright, golden presence announced the school's commencement and something I had anticipated for 12 years. But this would be different. Nothing would ever be the same.

At the last meeting of the City Council we were planning a December Christmas Carol Sing on the steps of the Capital building in downtown Detroit. We were planning for a large turnout and it was taking a lot of behind-the-scenes preparation. Knowing that this was my last meeting, when the meeting came to an end, I said my goodbyes to everyone, but as I turned to leave, Jim Gilman asked me if he could give me a ride home. We just had one car and my dad was going to come pick me up when I phoned him. So, thinking that Jim Gilman just needed me to do something before I left for school, in relation to our Christmas Carol Sing, I said, "Sure." I wouldn't need to look him straight on after all, he would be driving! As we drove in the car, there was no mention of the Carol Sing but he began to ask me all kinds of questions. Where was I going to school? When was I going to leave? What was my major? Was I going to date other guys? What about John? (John was a friend, when attending Grand River Baptist Church and we were often seen together).

After I addressed the intention to date while at college and that John was not in the picture, Jim asked this question, "Are you coming home for Christmas break? Would you be interested in going out with me on a Christmas date when you come home?" I was stunned! I was exploding inside! I couldn't believe my ears! With every bit of strength I could muster to contain myself, I managed to say with delicate response, "That would be very nice." It was almost in a whisper.

When I got in my house and didn't hear his car anymore, I exploded! I went running through the house, jumping and spinning, squealing and laughing! My father was sitting in his corner chair reading the newspaper. He pulled the paper down, looked overthe top of it, then slid it back up saying nothing! He didn't say a word! How could he be so calm when I felt like this, I thought! I was beside myself with disbelief and excitement!

How could I have been asked out on a date by Jim Gilman? How impossible that was to me! Where was this going? As I pondered this, I began to be tentative. I had given my life to full-time Christian service. Could marriage be in the picture? Was Jim Gilman that temptation that would supersede my commitment to make God my all in all? I remember my statement to the Lord, "I will do anything you want me to do, Lord. I will go anywhere and serve anywhere." I began to see this as a test of my commitment to the Lord. Jim Gilman was too much of a temptation for me. The Lord would need to remove him from me if it were not His Plan. I couldn't do it in the flesh. I was burdened, so I knew I needed to figure this out.

I asked the Lord to let me know at Christmas time if it were His Will for me to marry Jim, or if it were not. If it were not His Will for me, His Desire, then I asked the Lord to remove Jim Gilman from my life completely. "Please," I asked, "let me know on this Christmas break." I could then move forward either way; getting on with my life with no reservations, and know in my heart that I had been honest with God.

Cumberland College

Cumberland College was a small Christian college located in Williamsburg, Kentucky. It was particularly beautiful, especially in the Fall. The rolling hills were aglow with the brilliant hues of the season. The hills were like giant bouquets of orange, yellow and crimson flowers dispersed throughout patches of green, as if some trees were reluctant, competitively, to surrender to another season.

The large imposing colonial style buildings were stately, set on deep green lawns and held reminders of a different time, a time more genteel. The dorms, too, were the original southern mansion, colonial style. My dorm room felt unusually spacious. That was partly due to the 10-foot-high ceilings, and the large, tall window next to my bed that reached just up under the antique molding. All of this was very inviting, and I felt right at home. After all, this is where my parents went to college and my relatives were all around me. In my childhood, I had spent many summers in this little town. Maybe my mother and dad had the right idea for me!

I found myself quickly getting in the routine at Cumberland and I also found myself enjoying extracurricular activities. One activity that was provided for the Religion majors was the opportunity to minister to the small churches in the back hills of Kentucky. A team of students would be grouped together to present the Sunday morning worship service. This group was always special. There would be a ministerial student to present the sermon, someone to lead in congregational singing, someone to read the Scriptures, someone to sing special music, someone to lead in prayer. The pastors and their families in the churches were so gracious. After the Sunday morning worship service, we would be invited for Sunday dinner! What fun those times were. One time we all gathered around the piano and sang the old hymns for an hour. What sweet fellowship we had with these kind and humble servants of God in the hills of Kentucky. They blessed me.

Another extracurricular activity involved basketball. Basketball was the sport provided for the competitive young men at Cumberland. There were many on the team who were there on scholarships. The gymnasium and the annex building had been donated to the school under one condition – there would never be football. Due to serious injuries and concussions that surrounded football, this would be the stipulation. The gymnasium would be donated if football were banned. So, Cumberland's big game was basketball. There was no shortage of enthusiasm for our team. It seemed like everyone was involved. On the night before the big homecoming game, all students joined hands, forming a long winding human snake that began at the school and wound all through the town with an attempt to arrive at the bonfire with an unbroken line. If we succeeded without breaking our line, we were sure to win the Homecoming game. The fun was in the challenge!

On one occasion, one of the team members told me that I should try out for cheerleader. He said," You look like a farm girl with good strong legs." I didn't know if he were joking or not, but he said it with a perfectly straight face.

CHEERLEADERS . . . presenting Dr. Boswell the trophy which they won at the Kentucky Junior College Tournament for being the best there. Cheerleaders are: Barbara Foley, Mary Ann Cornett, Sallie Erwin, Lana Lewis, Paula Cox, and Sharon Siler. They were judged on cheering, sportsmanship, looks, and neatness.

I decided I would try out. I grew up without brothers, and my father was very bookish and had no interest in sports, so I had no one to introduce me at a young age to any sport. But now I found myself a cheerleader. My inexperience was evident on one occasion, when we were winning, but only by one basket. There wasn't much time on the clock. Then it seemed like from out of nowhere, a member of the other team appeared unguarded, racing the ball down the length of the whole court. Then, before the eyes of every amazed person in the gym, as the buzzer went off, he slam-dunked the ball to win the game! I was so impressed and shocked, I cheered for him! What a mistake! A cheerleader should never cheer for the other team. Duh! Of course, I was reprimanded by the cheerleader coach, but she didn't humiliate me anymore than I already was.

All these activities were fun things. The people I met and the things I learned were great, but the most prominent and reoccurring thought I had centered around Jim Gilman and the Christmas date. Each night, lying in my bed, I would look up through the tall, high window that displayed the beauty of the night sky. I would pause and just take it all in. What an Awesome God we have! Psalm 8 states, "When I consider Thy heavens, the Work of Thy Hands, the moon, the stars that Thou has ordained, what is man that Thou are mindful of Him? Or the son of man that Thou doest care for Him?" Yet, I had a strong sense that God did care for me. He had Spoken to me. He had Saved me. He had Invited me to give Him my life. He would Hear my prayer and Answer my plea concerning Jim Gilman. "Please, Dear God, let me know at Christmas time if I am to marry Jim Gilman." I told Him how happy I would be if it were His Plan, yet not my will, but His, be done.

The Christmas Date

The months rolled by. December was here and in all the months at Cumberland, I never felt homesick or missed my parents or felt the need to seek out my relatives. But as I was lying on my bed the night before I was to return home for Christmas break, thoughts of home poured over my mind. Suddenly, I couldn't wait to see my parents! Tears flooded my pillow. What will God reveal about my future when I get home? The Christmas date was upon me. Would Jim Gilman even remember that conversation in his car on the ride home from the council meeting? This would be the last night I would be coming to the Lord with my request before this star-studded window and its heavenly display. When I look through this window again, all these questions will be answered. "Thank You, Lord. I love You."

The Christmas Carol Sing

Seeing my parents was wonderful! There was so much to share. I felt the most important things to share were yet to come. The afternoon of the Christmas Carol Sing arrived. Would I see Jim Gilman there? Knowing that we would be standing outside on the steps of the Capital Building and it would be cold, I wanted to be warm. But, sometimes bundling up enough to be warm left the person warm but totally unrecognizable. So, I wore a cute furry hat and cute matching mittens. I wanted to look cute too.

Upon arrival at the Capitol Building, the streets and sidewalks were covered with youth. Youth were everywhere, and everyone was walking towards the steps. I couldn't see anyone except the person in the front of me. And I certainly didn't see Jim Gilman. As the crowd moved toward the steps, I eventually found myself on the very top steps, and from that vantage point, I could see all around. Then I saw Jim Gilman! He was walking briskly, here and there and everywhere, down off the steps, on the lowest part. Our paths never crossed.

When I got home, I took off my furry hat and cute little mittens and said to myself, "Well Sharon, there is your answer." At first there was a sting of disappointment, but then it immediately changed to thanksgiving. I had asked for an answer and the Lord had given it, and I was totally at peace with the answer. I was fine with the Lord's direction. Just at the moment I had completely surrendered to the

Lord's direction, the phone rang. The strong, handsome voice on the other end of the phone said, "Sharon, this is Jim. I didn't see you at the Carol Sing. Are you still fine with our Christmas date?" Wow! My heart jumped with anticipation! God was not finished yet!

The Christmas date lasted through the entire Christmas break! We went tobogganing, ice skating, had pizza parties, and everything was done with a group of friends from the church. My mother was always present at the end of the day to hear of all that we did, and she even opened our home to some of our gatherings. There was seemingly always something someone wanted to do together. In all of these "dates" Jim never did anything but take my hand in a gentlemanly fashion to aid me if it were appropriate.

As the end of the Christmas break approached, I realized that I still didn't know if the Lord wanted me to marry Jim. Did Jim just want someone to have fun with this break? That would be an answer. But when the time came for me to return to Cumberland, and my parents were going to drive me to the bus station, to my surprise, Jim asked if it would be alright if he could ride along with us. My mother was in the passenger seat, my father was driving, and Jim and I were in the back seat. Our conversation was not unique until Jim said, "I have always admired you during our time serving on the City Council together." It felt like my heart skipped a beat! I realized when Jim said these words, my answer from the Lord was coming, in the eleventh hour! The Christmas break was almost over. I responded by saying, "I have always admired you also." From that moment on, in the back seat of our car, with my parents hearing every word, we began to open up about our feelings for one another. I'm sure my mother was pleased. She had heard from the other mothers how special Jim was.

When I got on the bus, I was on cloud nine! I knew, without a shadow of a doubt, that Jim and I were going to be married! The Lord had answered my prayer within the time of the Christmas break! But did Jim know this? That would need to be God's work. The time on the bus for 500 miles flew by as I relived our 10-day time together. God was so Amazing! "Thank You, Thank You Lord."

Coming back to school with this incredible experience was overwhelming to me! I wanted to tell everyone! It wasn't just that I knew who was to be my future husband, but it was the remarkable way God has been so present and faithful in His relationship with me. I had given my life to Him; He gave back to me the desire of my heart! What a Kind and Wonderful Heavenly Father we have!

Two days after I arrived back to school (probably January 3rd) I was walking across campus towards the dining hall for breakfast. The morning was brisk but lovely and I was still basking in the wonder of all that had taken place. Long, golden shadows of morning were streaked across the ground and kissing the tops of the trees. I was full of joy so when one of the basketball boys caught up with me, I was bursting to tell him what had taken place. He had accompanied the Gospel Team as special music when we went to one of the churches in the hills of Kentucky. He was 6 feet 5 inches and he had a nickname, "Tiny." "Oh Tiny," I said. "Let me tell you what happened to me over Christmas break!" As I began my story, I looked up for a second to see someone coming straight towards me. Then I saw his big smile. It was Jim! I left Tiny standing there as I ran to Jim. How did he get here? How did he know where to find me? Did he drive all night? 500 miles is a long way! Was he tired? How long did he plan to stay? He began to answer my questions. He told me that when he got back to school, all he talked about was this girl in school in Kentucky. He wouldn't stop! So, to shut him up, several of his classmate buddies (GMI boys) drove all night, rotating drivers, arriving this morning and they would need to turn around and drive back that day, arriving that night. They were tired, but they were young, and it was an adventure. Jim asked me if they could plan to come on another visit again in February.

Mother To The Rescue

My mother did not want Jim Gilman to be treated half way! When she heard of the plans for a revisit February 18th, all the relatives were alerted! Aunt Alamae, my mother's sister-in-law and her daughter, Jo Florence, took over with the most extravagant, southern style, hospitality. The boys were invited to spend the night in their large colonial style home and wake up to eggs, bacon and grits, homemade biscuits and gravy. Dinner was served with platters piled high with southern fried chicken with all the trimmings. The warm welcome was so appreciated, and I'll never forget my family's involvement to help me. They certainly made the trip for the boys who helped drive, something worth making.

The weekend went by quickly. On Saturday morning we all drove to a beautiful vacation spot called, "Cumberland Falls." It was lovely, especially in the summer, but the excitement of Jim's visit made everything magical. Seeing Cumberland Falls with Jim was something I could never have imagined. That afternoon we all attended a basketball game. But most importantly, between these events, Jim and I were able to talk, and I began to realize that God had been working in Jim's heart too. What Jim was to say next would be the conclusion of my answered prayer. As we sat together on a large, cold rock on the Cumberland campus that February day, Jim casually stated, "It's just a matter of time and we are going to be married." Without hesitation, my response was simply, "I know." At

Cumberland Falls, out on the observation point, as Jim and I were watching the water splash and listening to its loud, thunderous roar, Jim kissed me with the sweetest little kiss...and the thunderous sound of the waterfalls was quite appropriate for the moment! After a long silence, we agreed to write one another every day.

What Just Happened?

After everyone left to return to Michigan, I began to process all that had taken place. God had very specifically answered my prayer! At the completion of the Christmas break, in the back seat of my parent's car, and on the bus ride back to Cumberland, I felt the Lord had revealed to me that Jim would be my husband! That was in response to my very specific request I had been making since September. On that rock, Jim verified my understanding when he didn't propose to me or ask me to marry him, he told me we would be married and that it was just a matter of time. I'm sure God put those very special words in his mind to say. They certainly demonstrated how attentively God heard my prayer. I had asked the Lord to let me know if I was to marry him. My response when I said, "I know" was in response to what God had given me to understand on the bus. This experience so strengthened my faith! God heard my every request and He was directing my life and He was working in Jim's heart, too.

However, this information changed the focus of my life; not a change in my focus on God, but a clearer focus and understanding of God's direction. I believed, without a doubt, that God had marriage to Jim in mind for me and that it was just a matter of time. But, how much time? I was ready to wait no matter how long God had for me to wait. He had been faithful to me to reveal what I had asked, so gratefully I would wait on His timing, just thrilled to have my path made clear! As I reasoned about the change marriage would mean, I realized that most likely it would involve a responsibility including family and children. I saw a conflict of interest. Both would demand total, serious commitment. Giving my life and devotion to full time work outside the home, even in Christian service, didn't seem right when our own children would have my tired hours of the day and care givers other than their real mother. It didn't seem right to Jim either. So, I determined to change my major to Psychology/Sociology with a

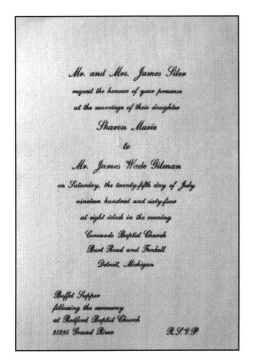

minor in Education. This would permit me to teach in public school if there would ever be a time before or after children. Jim and I also decided that my income would not be used to support the family. It would be disposable income only. We would live within the provision Jim provided and be content with that whatever that was.

The following Fall semester I left Cumberland and returned to my parent's home, living there with them until our wedding day 3 1/2 years later, and after graduating from University of Michigan. Jim also finished his fifth-year thesis at the same time and we both graduated in June 1964, he having an Industrial Engineering Degree, and I having a Bachelor of Arts in Education. We were married one month later, July 25, 1964. How long was the wait? God's perfect timing; 3 1/2 years.

Get Me To The Church On Time

Our churches, Grand River Avenue Baptist and Coronado Baptist, had provided many friends who had waited for the special day, along with us. And it wasn't void of prearranged bachelor party pranks. Two nights before the wedding, some of the friends in the wedding party captured Jim and drove him to Finely, Ohio and then, dropped him off on the road, in the middle of nowhere! Just as Jim could see what was happening, he grabbed Larry Grimes, who was one of the pranksters, and dragged him out of the car with him. The two of them were left there, challenged to find their way back home in time for the wedding! Surprisingly, even though these are two big men (Larry wore a size 14 shoe) people were not apprehensive about picking them up! Even though it took most of the night, they got back, tired but safe and sound.

The Two Become One Flesh

Our wedding was a beautiful, candlelit affair, casting an elegant glow on a mid-summer night. Having all our friends and loved ones around us all at one time to celebrate was special. But July 25th in Detroit, was hot! And air conditioners were not common then. Even though it was a beautiful candlelit wedding, and the sun had set a good time before, the night was hot, humid and still. As we stood before Pastor Noffsinger who was officiating, we'll always remember and laugh at the steady stream of sweat that ran off his nose forming a glistening trench on the front of his clerical robe.

But nothing could distract from the wonder of this moment! All of this was like a dream! The Lord was faithful to bring to pass all that He had told me 3 1/2 years ago. Those prayers I brought before the Lord at that tall, star spangled night window in my dormitory room at Cumberland were answered and the confidence in God's leading will last for a lifetime. Jim was to be my husband!

Those seemingly insignificant events that took place in my young teenage years contained the foundation for this moment in time. Martha, my dear sweet friend who saw I needed Jesus, when I was 13 years old, led me to a series of events that brought me to the most important decision I would ever make, and I gave my life to my Loving Savior Jesus Christ. I surrendered all my life to Him. From that point on, every path He guides me on is fragrant with His

Loving Kindness and Truth. This was God's will and direction for our lives; to journey through life together. To see the fulfillment of all that the Lord had shared with me those 3 1/2 years ago was now becoming a completed reality. Here Jim was now, standing before God and witnesses pledging his life and love to me. We were committing "until death do us part." Where would the Lord lead us? We two now will be one. Now I wasn't asking God to have only my life, but Jim's too. What happens to each of us happens to the other. And... I was now to be a married woman! In my new role as a wife, God would direct my life within the counsel of His Word as Jim's wife.

How thankful I was that we were both bringing our personal relationship with the Lord into our marriage. As our marriage continued through the years, that relationship with the Lord became a gift that God gave to each of us to give to the other. However now we were just beginning! The joy of this celebration was so evident! We listened intently to the Pastor's powerful words of commitment and selfless love. We pledged our lives to one another and faithfulness until death would part us. "Thank You Lord for Your faithfulness to bring this all to pass! May we serve You together according to the calling You have on our lives."

Psalm 37:3-5 "Delight yourself in the Lord and He will give you the desires of your heart. Commit your ways to Him. Trust in Him and He will do it."

Pretty Little Brick Houses

Pretty little brick houses, on a winding street with neat little yards, and a large weeping willow tree in the back yard. I had never seen a neighborhood like this before, but this was the vision that kept coming to my mind as Jim and I sought to purchase our first house.

We weren't looking for this, as if this were a vision that had to be fulfilled. It was just a reoccurring image that would come to my mind occasionally, unannounced. We had been advised that it was more profitable to invest in a small, starter house than it was to rent because to rent meant that each month, "one was putting money in a bucket with a hole in the bottom!" There was nothing to show for it except yesterday's memory of space to live in. However, when one purchases a home, the money goes into the purchase of the house which can possibly be money recovered, if sold.

This made sense to Jim and me, even though our friends who had married before us, had rented a year or so first. Jim only had $500 in his savings and I had nothing. But he was automatically employed at General Motors, as an engineer having graduated from their institute, so income would be steadily coming in. I learned this is important when applying for a loan. We eventually found a home for just the right price, $13,500.

We found it just at the right time. The closing and move-in day was a week after we returned from our honeymoon. Jim's parents, on vacation during that week interval, offered their empty home to us. Once again, the Lord's timing was our blessing. The home we found was a pretty little brick house, on a beautiful, winding street, lined up with other pretty little brick houses with neat little yards; but it was different than the other houses. It had a large weeping willow tree in the back yard, just as I had envisioned. Everything was exactly as I had imagined! This was astonishing to me! I think the Lord just wanted me to know that He was Present in all we did. "Thank You, Lord!"

When Jim and I moved in the first week in August of 1964 we took great delight in making our new home ours. We painted the living room walls with a soft suede, olive green. We put in new gold carpet and a new, soft, green couch. We found a floral arm chair that repeated the varying greens, gold and orange. I filled a tall, graceful, pottery type, orange vase with three large, artificial, brilliant orange and gold flowers. I painted a large, long, bold picture of various, interesting containers and hung it over our new couch. Those were the colors of the '60s and we were in style! It looked like a room set in a model home! And we were delighted and grateful for that!

Our bedroom was another focus. During our three and a half year wait to be married, while we were finishing school, we had acquired some old antique pieces of bedroom furniture. The bed had a very high headboard which was typical of that era. Jim cut it down so that it could be in proportion to the other pieces. He loved wood working, so with him as the boss, we refinished the furniture with antique white and gold trim. Our finished product was stunningly beautiful! Aunt Ree thought it so lovely, she did the same to their bedroom set! All of this was done in the basement of my parent's home when I returned home from Cumberland. After it was finished, it waited there in the basement for this day. It was our wedding bed. It looked so rich with the deep, royal blue spread and matching drapes against the stark white. We were grateful for the many wedding gifts, too. What a privilege to start our lives together with so much! Everything was new to us and it was very exciting.

What? Where?

Our first year living in our new home was filled with new adventures. I took my first teaching position in Livonia, Michigan at John F. Kennedy Elementary in the second grade, and I loved it. Jim was employed by Chevrolet, Detroit Gear and Axle, as an industrial engineer. Each Sunday we attended Jim's home church, Coronado Baptist (eventually Grand River Baptist and Coronado Baptist merged). Many of our longtime friends attended there, and even both of our sets of parents attended with us. We were in close driving distance to each of their homes. Our parents were so very happy for us. We were ready to spend a lifetime there. It was really sweet being surrounded by all those precious friends and family and living in our own home enjoying one another as husband and wife.

But the Lord had other plans for us. Jim's company offered him a position in Saginaw, Michigan, which was about a three-hour trip from Detroit. This was August of 1965. We had been in our home exactly one year and it seemed like we had just moved in! "What? Where?" was my first response, when Jim approached me with this information but as I listened to him, I saw that Jim felt that this was an opportunity for him to progress in his career, so we should consider it carefully. Should we leave all the comfort that we know, and step out into the unknown? We would know no one there. Family would be hours away rather than minutes. We decided this was the time in our lives, before children, to venture into the untried. Our pretty little house would go up for sale but before we could even get a sign up with a realtor and list it, one of our couple friends from church who had visited us had fallen in love with it and wanted to purchase it! The home had increased in value in the one year we lived in it, so we were able to sell it for $14,500. One thousand dollars more than we paid for it! We had lived for free! "Thank You, Lord, for giving us wise counsel. You are graciously blessing our finances and Your Presence and Goodness in our lives is obvious!"

Saginaw

In my early Christian walk, one thing I neglected was the study of God's Word. Oh sure, I knew Bible stories and I had listened to lots of preachers. My first year at Cumberland offered me the opportunity to study, but to really study with an adult mind, and read it regularly as a Christian discipline, I had never done.

I remember one summer when my folks went to Kentucky on one of their regular summer visits; my favorite cousins were out of state and I was essentially there in Kentucky without anyone my age (I think I was probably 11 years old). While my parents were occupied with the adults, I was really lost. But one of my older cousins, who was 18 years old, was home and invited me to stay with her. Her name was Jo Florence. I spoke of her earlier as the one who along with her mother, Aunt Alamae, entertained Jim's driver friends when he came to see me at Cumberland. I spent nights with her and followed her around each day as she went about her business. I discovered that she was very active in church and led a group of boys called, *Boys Ambassadors*. She was visiting their homes. She would talk to the parents and explain what she was teaching and doing with them.

One father kept trying to argue with her about what the Bible said. I remember how strongly she stated what the Bible did say. But she made her points without confrontation. Every night I watched her as she opened her Bible and read it. That really impressed me, and I wanted to make that a habit in my life also, but when I got back to Detroit, I tried to read my Bible, but I couldn't understand it, and I didn't seriously attempt again until I was in my late twenties.

Even though I knew the Lord had called me and I had given my life to Him, this was the condition I was in when I began my studies at the University of Michigan, majoring in Psychology. In my ignorance, I didn't understand that Psychology is one of the most godless studies one can pursue. Most who come out of a secular school with a doctorate in psychology are atheist. I was totally unprepared for the coming onslaught my neglect of the Word of God had left me. I had the same professor, Dr. Cohen, Head of the Psychology Department for all my Psychology classes. He knew I was a professing Christian and he seemed to want to catch me unable to defend what I believed.

I always had a response, but it was not very strong. I didn't realize how much this experience was affecting my faith, and how much I was trying to fit the information given in class to the information I had about God. Not even realizing what was happening, I prejudged God's Word without even having studied it. I began to believe that what I did know was not literal. It was only allegorical; in my arrogance, I had convinced myself that the Bible, in many cases, and I would pick and choose, was a symbolic representation. Jonah was not a real person…and not really swallowed by a whale. Nor were Adam and Eve real people. Nor was there a real Tree of Good and Evil nor the Tree of Life.

In my arrogance, I was fitting God into my own understanding, rather than accepting God's Infallible, Literal Word by faith. I didn't know that, as with other writings, the Bible does contain figures of speech, but I didn't realize that they must be interpreted for what they are and in light of their intended purpose. At the time, in my arrogant blindness, I didn't think my reasoning was at all contrary to God. I still knew I had given my life to Him. I still believed that Christ had died for my sins and saved me and that He had called me, and that

He was directing my life. But I soon discovered that this erroneous understanding that I was coming to was not to be believed by a true child of God! This was my spiritual condition as I entered into marriage and this continued to our move to Saginaw. God, in His Love for me, was going to set me straight.

Hopevale Baptist Church

Saginaw was very much like Detroit, except for no family nearby, and Jim and I were looking forward to repeating some of the things we had done there. First we purchased a home for $21,500. We poured our effort into decorating it as we had done with our first. I took a Second Grade teaching position at McBride Elementary, and Jim was challenged and motivated with his new position at Chevrolet Nodular Iron Foundry. But the most important thing we did was to immediately join a church, Hopevale Baptist, and begin to bond with the people who were there. Because we were sort of "newlyweds," married just one year, and the church was small, we were welcomed with open arms by many people.

We had a lot of good times with the people there. However, there were three families with whom we became very close. They were all about 15 years our senior and treated each of us like one of their children. They were mature Christians and offered Jim and me a wealth of wisdom, especially Jim. (Ever since I have known Jim, he has always had godly men who were glad to mentor him).

One of the men, whose name was Dick Cotton, was very active in the church, very dedicated to Christ and lived by his convictions and godly principles. He had a lovely wife, for whom I had great respect, and five children. He was a man who had a way about him that made others feel important. As well as all of this, he had become very successful in the jungle of the corporate world. He was vice president of a nationwide corporation, Wicks. And this world was exactly where Jim was headed. During Jim's education, he was told that to really get ahead and climb the ladder of the corporate world, he would need to socialize with the bosses, share meals and of course, drink socially. At the time we came to Saginaw, and with Jim just beginning his career, he was wrestling with this advice. Neither Jim nor I had been exposed to alcohol in our homes. Our parents both had the same belief—that a lifestyle without including it was best.

My father said to me one time when we were discussing alcoholic drinks, "Sharon, if you never take your first drink, you'll never be an alcoholic!" I always remembered that and never wanted to take my first drink. If it was good enough for my daddy, it was good enough for me. When Jim was confronted with this opposite consideration and shared it with Dick Cotton his response was clear! Never, never compromise one's convictions.

Dick had risen to the position of Vice President without ever compromising his Christian principles and convictions and was respected for them. He gave Jim suggestions as to what to do or say when the situation would arise. He told him he didn't need to carry a glass around to give a false impression. He said that when at an expensive restaurant with the "higher-ups" and was asked what he would like to drink, he would always ask for Catawba Juice which was a very expensive non-alcoholic grape juice. Jim embraced this counsel and was never tempted to deviate from it. Dick Cotton was a wonderful role model for Jim. He has continued to counsel Jim through the years, and I believe it was again evidence of the Lord's Guidance and Presence in our lives. "Praise You Lord, for Your church and the provisions You make for us through the Body of Christ."

However, Saginaw wasn't a place I was excited about. At least like that excitement which surrounded our first house. With our first house, the wait for our wedding day was fulfilled. The newness of marriage to the man of my dreams was in full bloom. The happiness we shared with our family and friends was at our fingertips. Our little home was a sweet and beautiful haven where we began to know one another as husband and wife.

A Strange Gloom

All of that was pretty hard to top! But I truly believed that the Lord was directing our lives, and this was the next step He wanted us to take, so I was ready to follow with bright and hopeful expectancy, with no reservations. Everything was going well; our marriage, our jobs, new friendships, church, but as we got settled in our new home and as the first few months went by, I began to experience a strange gloom. A darkness seemed to envelop me and reach down into my innermost being. This was something I had never experienced before. This heavy, black cloud was always present and along with it at times, was a sense of deep despair and hopelessness. I often couldn't sleep well and when I did sleep, I would awaken with disturbing dreams.

During the day I would find my mind preoccupied with destructive thoughts. The most tortuous agony of all of this was my destroyed relationship with God! I felt worthless, alone and existing without Him. I remembered the sweet times I called to Him, and He was always there and made His Gentle Presence known to me. I felt He was accepting others, but I was nothing and would never be anything but existing in this wicked separation from Him. I would call to Him, but he would not answer. He would have no part with me. I knew He was there to listen but the black, thick, sky of darkness hindered His response. In my cries out to Him I would say, "Oh Lord, I am nothing without You. I am worthless. This is what it feels like to be separated from You! It is misery and hopelessness! Please get rid of this wicked dark cloud that seems to smother all desire to live. Hope, worth, and joy, these things are only found in You!" Oh, how I wanted to escape this misery! I remember looking at the knives hanging on our kitchen wall and thought how they could be used to take my life.

After some time, in desperation, I asked the pastor from our church, Pastor Yost, to come to our home so I could share my agony and ask for prayer. I felt that I needed to tell someone that I could trust, and I felt that he was trustworthy. He listened intently and then said a sincere prayer for my healing. As the days went by, the days grew into weeks and weeks into months and the heavy load didn't move.

There was one message that came to my heart during this time. It was given to me when we were at a prayer meeting one evening. All of us present were sitting in a circle, sharing Bible verses. Of all the verses that were spoken that night, I believe the Lord sent one directly to my heart. It was found in Romans 8:38.

"For I am convinced that neither death, nor life, nor angels, nor principalities, nor things present, nor things to come, nor powers, nor height, nor depth, nor any other created things, shall be able to separate us from the love of God, which is in Christ Jesus our Lord."

This precious Word of God bathed my spirit with a confidence that the Lord would never separate me from His love! I was in Christ Jesus. He had called me, and I had given my heart and life to Him. He had given me an Eternal Security even unto death, that could never be revoked. This verse sank deep into my soul. Its supernatural power took hold and I internalized the truth of God's Word. The words were directly from God to my spirit. I quoted this verse often during the dark days that still lay before me and I became assured that even though it felt like I was separated from God the truth in God's Word is unalterable. He will never separate me from His love, no matter what I'm going through, and I had for the first time since it all began, a glimmer of peace.

One day when I was reading a magazine, I read an ad concerning mental health. The things described in the ad, the hopelessness and despair, identified some of the things that I was experiencing. A number was given saying that their professional services were provided by the state government and that they were free of charge. If I had any concerns and needed some help in this area, please feel free to give them a call. I called and made an appointment to meet with a psychiatrist.

I met with a lady once a week for several weeks. She listened to my situation each week and she prescribed some small red pills. I took the pills, but nothing changed. Due also to the regular feminine menstruation and possible problems in getting pregnant, the gynecologist that I had been seeing during the early part of our marriage prescribed birth control pills to help with regularity. I was also taking those. On one occasion during one of our weekly meetings, I suggested to the doctor that I throw all the pills away so that we could start a family. "Oh no!" the doctor shouted. "You are not able to deal with another change and major adjustment! Marriage, a new job, leaving your parents, and that familiar environment, new church, you will not be able to handle a new baby! That will compound your problem!" I wasn't so sure about that. I felt that it was not the situation that was my problem. I felt that it was something inside of me.

California, Here We Come!

Seemingly never-ending miles of prairie stretching as far as the pale blue horizon; miles of corn fields and wheat, farm houses and barns, breath-taking tall, craggy, majestic mountains that stood as immovable as the earth itself; bland and colorless deserts with silhouetted cactus standing in place, as if guarding it's dry, uninviting domain. These were the changing scenes as I gazed through the window of the passenger side of our convertible car. We were taking advantage of the free time allotted to me through the public school system – summer break!

This was the summer of 1966, one year after moving to Saginaw. Aunt Jo, my mother's sister, still resided in California and she and her husband, Uncle Clifton, had given us an open invitation to come and visit. Jim was always full of adventure. So, we camped out all the way, sleeping in a little pup tent, but eating all our meals in restaurants. It was an incredible experience for us! We would come to the campground after dark, not knowing what was around us. Then, when morning would come, and we opened the canvas flap on our tent, the panoramic display of the morning would burst through our senses; the brilliant morning sun, the clean fresh air, the sound of the earth teeming with life. One morning we threw open the canvas flap to find ourselves at the foot of the Tetons! Their mighty presence was indescribable! On this trip the created world in all its glory was displayed before my eyes for the first time in my life. What a Great God we must have! God's creation was more than I had ever known!

Upon arrival in California, we were given a warm and loving welcome from Aunt Jo, Uncle Clifton, and their teenage girls, Patty and Sandy. Besides being the most gracious, loving people and a joy to be around (which was entertainment enough) they made our trip filled with all that the entertainment capital of the world could offer. Aunt Jo arranged Disneyland, Knots Berry Farm, and the Ballet at the Rose Bowl performing Swan Lake. Aunt Jo had also made it possible for us to go behind stage and see the filming of the "Big Valley" which, at the time, was a very popular TV show. Barbara Stanwick and Linda Evans starred in the series and because of Aunt Jo's connection with her neighbor who worked there, they even took time to talk to us. We took it all in and were very much impressed with California! What a place! We had never seen so much in all our lives!

When it was time to leave, there were tears. When Jim and I pulled back onto the freeway heading east, I turned around and looking through the rear-view window, the Continental Divide was perfectly framed in the window. It was quite a beautiful sight. I bid farewell to the towering, impressive stretch, called the Continental Divide. I thought to myself, "I probably will never see you again." Little did I know, however, that next summer we would be packing our luggage once again!

On An Airplane?

Boy, was our luggage packed! Why did I think I needed to take seven different colored sweatshirts? Our luggage was packed to the very stuffed top. We had to sit on them to fasten the metal clips. And as cumbersome as it was, Jim and I wrestled everything out of the trunk of the car and hurried to the check in at the airport. The sights and smells were unfamiliar for this was my first flight! The thunderous roar of the jet airplanes taking off, the gaseous fumes, the hurry of the people, the sharp, crisp uniformed pilots and airline stewardesses, all painted a picture I had only seen in movies.

I really couldn't believe we had this opportunity to visit Europe! It was now the summer of 1967, the summer after our California trip. Larry Grimes, the GMI friend Jim had grabbed as he was shoved out of the car and dropped off in Finley, Ohio, on his bachelor party night, had accepted a position with General Motors Overseas Operations, in Lupton, England just outside London. He and his wife Linda, and new baby were living there and invited us to come and visit. He told us that we could make their home our headquarters. We were thrilled to accept! So here we were, anticipating new experiences that we had never imagined could have been reality.

Paris, the Eiffel Tower, the boat cruise on the Rhine River, eerie castles with spiraling peaks and weird gargoyles, elaborate, ornate cathedrals, the Champs De Le-Say, the Arc de Triumph, the gondola

boat ride in Amsterdam, the Changing of the Guard in London, Italy and the evidence of the Renaissance, seeing the Sistine Chapel, Michael Angelo's statue of David and the Pitta were some of the sights we saw. For me, the Colosseum in Rome was the most unforgettable. Just to realize that because of their faith in Jesus, multitudes of Christians were savagely torn apart by wild beasts or pitted against one another as gladiators until death freed them from their constantly living nightmares, all for the entertainment of man's twisted perversions. How many prayers of the saints were uttered within these catacombs? Today this huge broken-down monstrosity still stands as a reminder of mankind's depravity and how assuredly the pit of hell can envelop the human mind. God, have mercy on us!

Upon returning to the United States we went to visit our parents in Detroit. They wanted to see us after our big trip as "World Travelers!" Aunt Ree and Uncle Andrew were there to greet us also. This was August of 1967 and was the year that the riots in Detroit took place. As we visited our family on their front lawn we could see the smoke from the fire of the riot. It saddened us to see Detroit so gripped with discontent and destruction. From the time I ran home from school in fear as a child in the streets of Detroit, to this day 20 years later, things have come to this. What a lost world we live in. How different my life would have been if we had not moved away. Would I have made any difference?

A Weekend Escapade?

Our amazing July to August trip of four weeks in Europe, held memories that will never be forgotten, but the high stack of mail that had accumulated while we were gone brought us back to the reality of our lives in Saginaw. As Jim stood in our kitchen sifting through the mountainous pile of mail, he came across a letter from a job placement agency. Jim said that the places looking to hire engineers, send out these letters recruiting young graduates from General Motors Institute. They provide opportunities to interview for needed positions. Then he said, "We're not interested in that, are we?" I said, "No," If he was happy, I was happy. Then as he kept reading, he declared, "This opportunity is in Santa Monica, California with McDonnell Douglas and the interview is in November!" As he read, we learned that the interview was over a weekend. There was no obligation, and all expenses were paid! "Well," he said, "what a great opportunity to visit California again. It will be an all-expense paid trip, and we are not obligated to take the position. Shall we do it?" Jim questioned. "It all makes sense to me! Let's do it!" I exclaimed in a playful way.

When it was time for our trip, it was mid-November. In Saginaw the days were starting to become obviously shorter. The cold wind of late fall ushered in the beginning of winter. I was accustomed to the change of season, having lived in Michigan most of my life, but this time the heaviness and bleakness of dark, winter days was not as welcomed. The cloud of depression continued to hover over me for the two years we had been in Saginaw, and the thought of no escape plagued me. However, Jim and I were very active in our church and even volunteered to direct the youth group. We did many activities with the families with whom we were particularly close. I took some post graduate courses and did well and continued teaching every day.

One morning as I was getting ready for school, I was surprised when the phone rang. A Detroit radio station had said that Sharon Gilman from McBrite Elementary School in Saginaw, Michigan had been voted "Teacher of the Day." This was announced over several stations, even in Detroit, and it was an unexpected encouragement. The children and the parents at McBrite were wonderful people; they were the ones responsible for initiating the honor. They wanted me to know that what I was doing for their children was appreciated and hoped that this demonstrated their gratitude. I was humbled and grateful for them. Jim, too, was doing well in his position and was content at Chevrolet Nodular Iron Foundry. We both were ready to embrace another year. But the time for our California weekend getaway was here and things at home would be put on hold.

California, Here We Come, Again?

Our getaway trip was more important than we realized. What we at first believed was to be a little getaway became something that would affect our lives for a decade to come. From the very first moment we exited the Los Angeles airport, the contrast between Michigan and California was obvious. A waft of warm air gently greeted us, and flowers were in bloom. The days were becoming shortened, as in Michigan, but there wasn't a dread when the sun was setting with such radiant, warm colors. This was November. It felt like summer was still here. If our decision to move to California was based on the weather, I was convinced this would be a great place to live. But there was more.

When Jim returned from the interview, he was convinced that it was a great opportunity for him, professionally. The interview went very well. He told me that they made an offer and then made a second offer, one that he couldn't refuse. McDonnell Douglas would handle all the move – everything from the pieces of soap in our soap dishes to the trash in our waste baskets! With all of this, before we left to return to Saginaw, Aunt Jo wanted to show us some homes for sale.

Tall, high ceilings with windows and drapes to match, elegant, graceful stairways, plushy white wall to wall carpet, soft fluffy pillows, large master bedrooms, other spacious rooms each furnished and decorated with colors as bright and lovely as the California sunshine. These homes were what we saw as Aunt Jo directed us to areas that she thought would be of interest to us. Neither Jim nor I had ever seen homes like these before. These were model homes. Something very different than what we ever thought existed. Developers would come in and build model homes, and then sell a particular home based on what was chosen from the models. Lots were sold according to the model. These homes were staged like only Hollywood could do. It was all so inviting. Even the name of the development was attractive, "Porter Ranch." Were we going to live in Porter Ranch?

When we returned and shared all of this with our parents, they were very supportive. My father had been in California before he was married, to work in the oil fields. After returning to Kentucky and marrying my mother, he always wanted to go back. He was hoping Jim would get a transfer so that he and my mother could live there someday. Here was his opportunity and my mother was happy to comply. After all, not only would Jim and I be there, my mother's sister, Aunt Jo and her family would be there too.

With Jim's new salary, and the sale of the Saginaw home, which had increased $1000 in value in the two years we had lived in it, we could afford to live in Porter Ranch! Before we left California, while in the sales office, we picked out a model we liked on a cul-de-sac lot. This home would be completed in the spring. Jim was to be on the job in California late January 1968 so there would be a gap of three months waiting for the completion of the house.

Even before arriving in California, Aunt Jo and Uncle Clifton graciously offered their family room and hide-a-bed couch to us as an interim solution to the time it would take to find a home in which to relocate. We accepted happily, but now were very concerned that we would wear out our welcome in the three months. We determined that we would eat all of our meals out, except breakfast (only cereal) and it was eaten only after everyone had left for work or school. When Jim would come home after work, we would immediately go out for dinner and then shop for things to go into our new home, returning just a little before bedtime. This arrangement worked well, and the time was filled with cherished memories of loving family.

Fed Up!!!

Jim's heavy, rhythmic breathing as he lay next to me in Aunt Jo's hide-a-bed, told me he was resting well. How I envied his ability to sleep and greet the new day rested and motivated with a feeling of well-being. I had been awake since before dawn, troubled with weird imaginations and haunting depression. During our two years in Saginaw, I had been struggling with it and now I realized that it was going to continue to follow me. The feeling of isolation and hopelessness covered my whole body. Finally, I got up and found myself pacing anxiously, uncontrollably wringing my hands. About that time, Jim awakened. Understandingly, he comforted me and told me not to worry. We would find another psychiatrist to help. The thought of another psychiatrist only made me realize how little help that had been. Nothing helped! With that, I ran into the bathroom and grabbed the container of little red pills and threw them in the garbage. I also took the birth control pills on the little round disk and threw them away also, shouting, "And I'm fed up with these pills!"

In the days that followed, I went about the business of applying for a teacher's position in the Los Angeles School system. The gathering of my records was time consuming. A list of schools attended, degrees acquired, grade point averages, former positions, letters of recommendation and physicals all needed to be provided for consideration. Days and weeks went by as this process continued. I was hoping to be hired as early as February, but I could see that was just not going to happen. However, during this time something was different. Although it was a very gradual realization, I noticed that there were no deep periods of heaviness and hopelessness.

The last episode occurred that morning I threw the pills away. It couldn't have been the red pills because I had gone to the psychiatrist while I was having the trouble and I had not had the pills yet. I had taken the birth control pills for the entire two years. My mother had told me not to take birth control pills. This was mid-sixties. The pill was new. The pill had not been tested with time and the balance of estrogen in a woman's system is in a delicate balance. I didn't heed her advice because the doctor had prescribed them. However, I never took birth control pills again and I have never experienced the agony of that kind of depression again!

For whatever the cause, I was allowed to experience that miserable time of my life. It humbled me. The most difficult thing about the time, was my feeling of separation from the Lord. My walk with Him had been so close. But knowing how awful it was to feel separated emphasized my need and desire for Him all the more. I was so grateful to Him for bringing me through it. I felt humbled, and any pride or egotism that existed within me, directly after my secular education, in psychology, was gone! I realized fully that I am nothing without the Presence of God in my life. I also had a new perspective on God's Word. How dare I reduce the precious Word of God to trite allegories. I began to understand how ignorant of the Scriptures I had been. I would never doubt again that every Word in the Scriptures was true in its literal sense unless obvious otherwise.

"Teach me, Oh Lord! May I be pliable in Your Hands!"

1 Peter 5:10 states, "And after you have suffered for a little while, the God of all Grace, Who called you to His Eternal Glory in Christ will Himself Perfect, Conform, Strengthen and Establish you."

I have hidden in my heart, Romans 8:38, 39 "For I am convinced that neither Death nor Life, nor Angels, nor Principalities, nor Things Present, nor Things to come, nor Powers, nor Height, nor Depth, nor any other Created Thing, shall be able to separate us from the Love of God, which is in Christ Jesus, our Lord."

Los Angeles City Schools

The mail was once again piled up in my hand as I checked to see if the Los Angeles School System had sent me any correspondence. It had become a habit for me to go expectantly through the mail only to be disappointed. It had been certainly enough time, I thought, as I looked through this new batch of mail. Then, just as I had come to the last business envelop, there it was — a letter from the Los Angeles City Schools, addressed to Mrs. Sharon Gilman.

I tore open the envelope and began to read. They had found in my application some information that would need further clarification. They were concerned about my response to the question, "Are you taking, or have you ever taken any psychiatric medication?" I had answered all questions to the best of my ability, not at all thinking it would give any concern. I never would have concealed information or lied about anything. No matter what the truth was, it needed to be stated. As a Christian, I had no other option. They wanted an interview with me to determine if the concerns were too great. If they were, they would find it impossible to hire me. I was shocked and worried! Frantically, a multitude of questions loomed over me! Because of this, would I be unable to teach school here in California? Maybe this would keep me from teaching anywhere! Was this God's plan, for me to be educated as a teacher and then be led a different direction? I must trust God, but what was I to do? I was not wanting to tell Aunt Jo. What would she think? What would her girls think?

Or Uncle Clifton? I knew Jim and I could figure things out...but all of this was humiliating! Then I realized that I did need to confide in Aunt Jo. She had been teaching in the Los Angeles Schools for many, many years. She was level-headed and wise. She would not belittle me in any way, so I "swallowed my pride" and looked for a good opportunity to talk to her.

As I sat at Aunt Jo's kitchen table, I poured out every detail of the situation. I told her that I had not been hindered at all, in performing as a competent teacher and hoped that this would not be blown out of proportion. I told her of my successes while teaching at that time. Then, she began to tell me what to do.

The interview was a couple of weeks away, so there was still time. She told me to ask for letters of recommendation from people who knew me and witnessed my successes during those years, like Pastor Yost and the principals of the schools where I taught. I should include the transcripts showing straight A's for the post graduate classes that I took. She told me to make sure everything was clearly dated, so that they can see the outstanding productivity of that time. I followed Aunt Jo's advice.

As the day of the interview approached, I called ahead and got directions to the administration building. I didn't want to be late or do anything on my part to cast doubt on my abilities or character. When I arrived at the administration building, and as I walked up to the entrance, to my surprise I had a peace and confidence. I really think that after reading all the letters of recommendation and seeing the records, it persuaded me of my own abilities! After identifying myself to a friendly lady at the main desk, she led me to the meeting room. It was a large room and the chairs were in a circle seating about 15 stern looking people. There was not a smile on any of their faces, as I was invited to sit down in one of the chairs in the circle. However, I was still not intimidated and when they asked me questions, I answered as honestly as I could without being too descriptive. When it seemed that all the questions were answered, I took out the letters and the records and I began to pass them out, one at a time, each person given the opportunity and time to read each one. All was quiet until the last was read. Then the interview was over, and they said that I would be hearing the results within the week. I left feeling satisfied that I had done all that I could have done. Now the Lord would do His work...whatever was His plan.

Yes! Within the week, I did hear the results of the interview! I was offered the Second Grade full time position beginning March of 1969 for the Los Angeles City Schools. I taught there until June of 1969. Teaching there was a delight, but the struggle which took place prior to being hired will never be forgotten.

Boxes, Boxes, Boxes!

Moving day into our new home was quite a revelation. We had so much stuff! Where did everything come from? There were boxes piled ceiling high in our three car garage; in the bedrooms, living room, kitchen and every other room in the house. How could we have accumulated so much? Jim and I dove into the task of unloading the boxes and putting things in their places. I began with enthusiasm but was soon overwhelmed, so I attempted to narrow my focus and begin in the master bedroom closet. That was a smaller area and less overwhelming, but in just a matter of minutes, I found myself getting sleepy. The brand new, pretty, white, carpet was so soft and warm and smelled so good and new; I couldn't resist curling up and taking a little cat nap. Jim came up to see how I was doing only to find me sound asleep! My nap had lasted an hour and not one box was unpacked!

I remember the same heavy desire to sleep when we stayed at Aunt Jo's. When Jim and I would go shopping each evening, my greatest pleasurable anticipation, each evening was to sleep in the car while Jim did the shopping. Jim was so gracious. He never made me feel awkward about this or question me about why I was sleepy all the time or why I didn't do my share of the unpacking, or why I didn't enjoy picking out things for our new house. He always used encouraging words and made me feel like this "sleeping thing" just wasn't anything important. "Thank You, Lord, for giving me a loving, considerate husband."

This sleeping problem never really interfered with anything important except for one morning when I had arrived at school early. I had only begun with my second-grade assignment and I wanted to make a good impression. I had made the day's plans for the children and I sat at my desk waiting expectantly for the children to come in. As I sat there, I felt that heavy, familiar, sleepy wave come over me. I thought I could rest just for a minute, so I let my forehead drop flat down on my desk. I don't know how long I was in this position, but I was startled by hearing the outside door to my room, open with a sweeping whoosh! I popped my head up just in time to see my principal coming through the door! I don't remember what he said to me. I was so surprised and embarrassed. Had he seen me sleeping on the job? We talked for a minute, then he left. I was totally embarrassed! The teacher before me had mounted a mirror on the back of a cupboard door, and as I glanced up, there was my reflection staring at me with the telltale sign on my forehead...a bright red circle where my head had rested on the desk!

This occurrence was never mentioned and my remaining time with the Los Angeles Schools continued without any other incidents. After observing all these strange and inappropriate times to drop off to sleep, Jim and I discussed the possible reasons why these waves of sleep would come upon me. Sometimes going from one time zone to another takes time to adjust and set new sleep patterns. We were now living in a new time zone. Sometimes change in sleep patterns surface when a medication is stopped, especially if stopped abruptly. I had abruptly stopped the little red pills. The sleepy episodes finally did pass, and a newness of life really flooded my soul!

California Living

Living in California was a new experience! Everything was beautiful and new, everything from a new climate, new home, new church, new jobs, to being near family again! Jim was happy with his new position at McDonnell Douglas, in Santa Monica. I continued to teach. I had a shaky beginning, but now there was just so much for which we could be grateful. The Lord had provided more than we could have ever imagined! There just wasn't anything else we could desire. In our new Porter Ranch home, we even had a beautiful, sparkling swimming pool. But there was just one thing missing. We wanted a baby!

We were going into our fifth year of marriage and because we had been unsuccessful previously, for whatever the reason, we decided to get a fertility doctor to help. We did everything the doctor told us and the results were always the same. Finally, I asked the Lord if maybe we were to adopt a child. What was the Lord's will? Once again I looked into my heart. Did I really want the Lord's will? I laid everything before Him and asked, "Lord would You please allow us to conceive by January of 1969 if you want us to have our own biological child? If You want us to adopt a child, let us continue to be barren." The Lord had always been faithful to me when I asked for direction. Now, in faith, I was asking for this. I was still teaching in Los Angeles City Schools and knew this would be my last teaching assignment if I were to become pregnant. A lot of things would change.

The weeks went by and there was no baby. I was beginning to think that the Lord had adoption in mind. As I lay on the examination table in the doctor's office, ready for the routine exam, I understood it was the first week in January. As the examination continued I had perfect peace that the Lord would do His perfect will, no matter what the outcome of my request. Suddenly, the doctor pushed back his wheeled examination chair, and with a deep breath declared, "Mrs. Gilman, you are going to have a baby!" Wow! It was January 6, 1969 when Kimberly Michelle Gilman was conceived. She was born October 1, 1969. Exactly nine months later and to our surprise, 21 months later, her little baby brother, Kevin James Gilman, was born, without the help of a doctor! The Lord had blessed us with two beautiful children! I was 29 years old. "Thank You, thank You, Lord for once again letting Your Presence be seen and felt as I called upon Your Name. You prove Yourself True, Faithful and Loving over and over throughout my life! May You have all the Glory and Praise. May our children grow up to know You and know Your Presence as You have made known to me!"

The Temptation

As I stood before the window at my kitchen sink making breakfast, I was watching and laughing at our children playing in our California backyard. Kevin, now two years old, was providing special entertainment for Kim and me. He was in the grassy yard running and squealing, laughing hilariously, wearing only his diaper, which was barely hanging on. It was already wet and full from the long night, but that didn't deter his fun that morning. He would run to each sprinkler head that was squirting, spitting, and struggling to come on, sit on it and watch and feel the water explode beneath him. Each sprinkler head was just as much fun as the one before and his laughter proved it. He would race to each one, attempting to catch each, just before it would burst through. This had become a morning ritual! The sprinkler system was on a timer and when it came on, making loud hissing and sputtering noises right under Kevin's bedroom window, it was his alarm clock. He would quickly climb over the bars of his crib, run downstairs with great anticipation to catch the sputtering water under his squat. If we got up in time, Kim and I could see this spectacle every morning, otherwise, Kevin enjoyed the water works all by himself. Our children were certainly a joy to us!

Everything was perfect! We even had our perfect family. I felt so secure, so happy. It was 1974. We had been living in California for six years. The soft carpet, and handpicked furniture chosen just to fit in the particular places, enough bedrooms for each child to have their own room, even an extra bedroom for guests, the sparkling swimming pool in our side yard, the flowers and sunshine, were all a part of this new perfect world. I knew with all my heart that God had granted me all these things and I was totally unworthy! Then the Lord spoke to me in my heart. He said, "IF I ASKED YOU TO GIVE UP THIS HOUSE IN FAITH, WOULD YOU DO IT, NOT KNOWING WHAT WAS TO COME?" I stopped in my tracks. A deep heaviness flooded my heart as I thought about His question. Then I realized that I was hanging on too tightly to these material things. I could not honestly admit before God that I would give it up in my heart with faith. All day long I struggled with myself. Later in theafternoon I began to see how foolishly I was thinking. To trade God's will for this perishable material thing is completely a temptation from Satan!

Nothing is more Wonderful and would bring more Joy than to rest in the arms of His Perfect Will and His Embracing Loving Kindness. If that meant giving up the house, so be it! I had won the battle! I was convinced! I would never trade God's will for anything, knowing by faith and experience, that He Loves me, and He has Created me for His Loving and Gracious Purposes. I belong to Him! I have surrendered my all to His Will.

Just about that time, I heard Jim come in downstairs from work. I ran down to meet him. As I looked at him, he didn't seem himself. He seemed a "little off." I questioned him. Then he said to me that he was told today that his job was moving from Santa Monica to Long Beach (an hour and a half drive away) and that we would need to move or find another job! This was totally unexpected! But the Lord had prepared me, so I shared with him the struggle I had during the day, as well as the outcome. The Lord was in control! I was completely ready to do whatever we needed to do, with Faith and Trust in God. We would wait on Him for Guidance. "Thank You, Lord, for preparing me so that I could be a strength to Jim and not an upset wife, unable to give up material things. You knew that I needed to deal with this today. Thank You, Lord! Once again, Your Timing is always Perfect!"

Canoga Park Baptist Church

One of the first things Jim and I had done when we moved to a new location was to determine in which church we were to worship. That was top priority, because we both recognized that the Scriptures were clear. We would be out of His will if church and worshiping corporately were not a part of our lives. We would hinder God's work in us and through us.

We decided to join Canoga Park Baptist. It was very alive and friendly, and the pastor was a gifted evangelist. He preached with compelling persuasion to accept Christ as Savior and the power of the Holy Spirit, was evident. The church was growing so rapidly, the need for a bigger facility was becoming increasingly more obvious. A perfect property became available that had been owned by Bob "Bazooka" Burns, a popular entertainer during the 1940s. He had passed away and his sprawling mansion on six acres was purchased by the church. It was to be a temporary place while plans for building an accommodating sanctuary would move forward. This was the position of the church when Jim and I joined.

We joined with gusto! Jim took on the responsibility of renovating the buildings to facilitate classrooms for Sunday School. Since we had our little children in the nursery area where there was a leaky roof, right over where the cribs were meant to go, Jim started there. He recruited the men of the church, organized them and went to work.

It seemed like everyone in the church was on board! My time while living with Judy introduced me to drawing and painting so I helped by painting large murals on the nursery walls, as well as on several of the walls in the primary classrooms. The area with the leaky roof became a focal point. Here I painted a large Noah's ark, animals and all, in a very soft lavender, delicate turquoise and white. The room was so

lovely and peaceful; a far cry from the neglected state it had been in. From the nursery, the crew went to the mansion itself, with hammers and saws, dry wall repairs from floor to ceiling, plaster and paint. Even the grounds needed attention and that was covered too.

Jim was always the first on the job and the last to leave. When the project was finished, everything was as fresh as brand new! Meanwhile, as we were loving and raising our babies we were using our spiritual gifts by serving in the church. Jim served, at various times, as a trustee, an elder, and when the time came, on the pulpit committee to find a new pastor. I served as the superintendent of the Children's Sunday School and taught where it was needed.

"And He gave some as apostles and some as prophets and some as evangelists, and some as pastors and teachers, for the equipping of the saints for the work of service to the building up of the body of Christ..." Ephesians 4:11

I have thought it was interesting that the Lord laid on my heart to serve as a Christian Education Director when I was 13 years old. That has been where the Lord has put me informally in all our church experiences.

Bob Jones

As the days went by, the time for transferring Jim's work from Santa Monica to Long Beach drew near. But he had made up his mind. He decided that he did not want to move to Long Beach, and he would rather look for another job. How long could we wait for him to find another position? Would we have enough to sustain us until he could find another job? Little did we know, but the service that Jim had been doing for the church was being observed by a man by the name of Bob Jones. He held an executive position at Atomic International which was a part of Rockwell Corporation. He told Jim that he had been impressed with his ability to manage men, evidenced by the leadership he demonstrated in completing the renovation of the Bob Burns property. He noticed his ability to lead the pulpit committee and he noticed his consistent testimony throughout the years we had attended Canoga Park Baptist Church. He wanted Jim to apply for a position at Atomic International that would incorporate his experience, leadership and strengths.

With Bob Jones' recommendation and influence, Jim was hired immediately. This new position was only 20 minutes from our home! "Lord, You are constantly working to do wondrous things in my life as well as Jim's. The blessings overflow when one is equally yoked with his or her life's mate. May I have my eyes open to always praise You and give You the Glory for causing these things to come to pass! You are so Faithful!"

Betty

Jim and I were so blessed by the people at Grand River Avenue Baptist, Coronado Baptist, and Hopevale Baptist. Once again, we were blessed by the people at Canoga Park Baptist. Now Bob Jones' influence in our lives was far-reaching. It reached all the way throughout Jim's 30-year corporate world career and through the years he was promoted to higher management positions. I realized more and more how the Lord works through one another in the body of Christ. Maybe that's one reason He tells us not to forsake the assembling of ourselves together. Just one suggestion or comment from a faithful believer can play an important part in our well-being far into the future.

"Thank You Lord for the Church, the Body of Christ! Your Plans for all things are for our Good and Your Glory."

Betty was an older lady whose children had grown and were married, and she also attended Canoga Park Baptist Church. One day, I invited her over for lunch. During her visit, we talked about child rearing and various challenges in raising children. Suddenly, she said, "You and Jim ought to go to a conference that will be held a few weeks from now." She explained a little about it and it sounded interesting, so later that day, when Jim came home from work, I shared with him what Betty had told me. We decided to go. It was an all weekend conference, so my mom and dad took care of the children. They lived only 20 minutes away and always looked forward to being with their grandchildren. This conference, presented by Bill Gothard, was called Basic Youth Conflicts. We were told to bring our Bibles and they provided workbooks. It began on a Friday night and continued all day Saturday. It was held in Long Beach Sports Arena holding thousands of people and it was packed!

There were many important subjects covered but the two that I would like to share are forgiveness and submission.

Forgiveness

"Make every effort to live in peace with all men and to be holy: See to it that no bitter root grows up to cause trouble and defile many." Hebrews 12:14-15

"If you are offering your gift at the altar and there remember that your brother has something against you, leave your gift there in front of the altar and first go and be reconciled to your brother, then offer your gift." Matthew 5:23-24

When this subject was presented at the seminar, I decided that I would follow Bill Gothard's suggestion and ask the Lord to bring to mind any relationship that I should reconcile. Immediately upon this request the Lord brought to mind a young woman at church. Her name was Kay. Because she and her husband and children were in about the same place in life as Jim and I were, we found much in common and had become friends. However, the closer we became the more uncomfortable I was in her presence! She was beautiful, witty and full of fun! She was loud and drew attention to herself. Even Jim seemed to join in the laughter. The longer time went by, I grew to feel more and more insignificant and awkward. So, when the Lord brought Kay to my mind, I realized that I was jealous of her. Now that this had been revealed to me, I realized also that I needed to see that no bitter root grow up. I felt that bitterness surely could begin. It could cause trouble and defile many. I even saw that it could bring conflict between Jim and me. I began to feel an urgency. Before I made any offering to Him,

I needed to confess my offense to God and her. I needed to quickly get this resolved.

Now this would be the hard part, humbling myself before her. I didn't see her often. In my uncomfortable state I thought maybe God would never give me the opportunity to face her so that I would not need to do this hard thing. But I had sincerely confessed my offense to the Lord and committed myself to approaching her when I saw her. I would ask her to forgive me for the jealousy that I had harbored toward her. I realized that it was ugly and something of which God had convicted me. To admit that something this ugly was in me, drew me to my knees. How imperfect I am!! I really didn't look forward to verbally admitting these things, especially to Kay, but the next day was Sunday. The weekend of the conference had just ended and all of it was fresh on my mind. Would I see her then tomorrow at church? As I thought about this, however, it would be very unlikely that I would even see her! She attended the first service with her family and Jim and I attended the second. Our paths usually did not even cross on Sundays. But the Lord is a Great God, and if this were very important He would make the way.

The next day, I awoke with the anticipation of living out my commitment to the Lord. Jim and I were totally filled with information we had received from the weekend seminar. I felt I was bursting inside with all the truth of God's Word. I was so eager to live it out and the beginning was with this new concept of asking forgiveness. In my pride, however, this was hard for me.

As we were pulling into the church parking lot on this bright Sunday morning, everything was quiet and no one was in sight. The cars were lined up in their spaces like mounds of rocky metal waiting in quiet slumber. The first service was still in process and it seemed that every parking space was filled. Jim drove slowly and quietly looking for a place to park. Suddenly, turning around at the end of the lined cars, in an attempt to check once again for an empty space, a child stood in the middle of the parking lot. She was crying! I jumped out of the car and ran to her. To my surprise, it was Kay's 7-year-old daughter! She told me that she wanted her mom, but she didn't know how to find her! I knew that her mother attended the first service, so I believed that she was in the worship service. Taking the child to the sanctuary, I looked through the windows on the sanctuary doors, and I could see Kay seated about half way down in an aisle seat.

As I was leading the child down to her mother, I realized that God was leading me face to face with Kay! He was enabling me to exercise my commitment! Forgiveness is very important to the Lord! God had miraculously placed Kay's little girl, literally in my path, in an empty parking lot, so that no one else would come to her aid, and timed it perfectly for our encounter!

Pushing the windowed swinging doors of the sanctuary open, I quietly walked to Kay with child in hand. Stooping down at the end of the aisle, I explained I had found her daughter in the parking lot. Then I told her I had another matter. I looked Kay straight in her eyes and told her that I had been harboring jealousy in my heart toward her and I wanted to ask her forgiveness. With clear and sincere words, I said, "Will you please forgive me for holding jealousy in my heart toward you?" I waited for her response. She was rather bewildered, but after gathering her composure, she said in the most tender voice, and with a great big hug, "Oh, of course I will!" I turned and not wanting to disturb the service any more than I had, quickly left the sanctuary. I was set free!! That jealousy never returned! I began to embrace Kay as a beloved sister in the Lord.

"Oh Lord, how Faithful You are to demonstrate how important asking for forgiveness is. I will never forget this lesson. Thank You for enabling me to do Your will. I am free because You are in my life!" I also will remember Betty and how significant the people in the Body of Christ are. I learned through Betty about this seminar! It has impressed me throughout my entire life.

Submission To Authorities

Bill Gothard took us through important major conflicts in life and revealed what God's Word said about those conflicts. Another conflict that he addressed concerns authority.

He gave us this hypothetical situation: Suppose you feel as though you have met the girl of your dreams. You are wanting to ask her to marry you. From your perspective she has all the qualities that make her just perfect. Your parents think that she is wonderful, but they don't think you should marry her, at least for now. Raise your hand if you would marry her anyway. Hundreds of hands went up all over the stadium. Even though there are many variables that could be added to this hypothetical situation, the speaker would lead us to the principle in Scripture that would give direction.

Ephesians 6:2-3 tells us, "Obey your parents in the Lord for this is right. Honor your father and mother which is the first commandment with a promise, that things may go well with you, and you may live long on the earth." This honor is given to parents so that things will go well with them. Parents can have another perspective that can only be revealed in time. But obedience to this admonition brings blessing.

Romans 13:1 says, "Everyone must submit himself to the governing authorities, for there is no authority except that which God has established. The authorities that exist have been established by God."

"Submit yourselves for the Lord's sake to every authority instituted among men. Whether to the king, as the supreme authority, or to governors, who are sent by Him to punish those who do wrong and to commend those who do right." I Peter 2:13

"Slaves submit yourselves to your masters with all respect, not only to those who are good and considerate, but those who are harsh." I Peter 2:18 (This can apply to employers.)

"Wives, submit to your husbands as to the Lord. For the husband is the head of the wife as Christ is head of the church. Now as the church submits to Christ so also wives should submit to their husbands in everything." Ephesians 5:22

God has provided the answers and direction for all of the issues in life. As we search the Scriptures and make it a part of our lives, we will be led by His Spirit and know what is pleasing to Him and what is His Good and Perfect Will.

"His Word is a Lamp unto my feet and a Light unto my path, and I will hide His Word in my heart that I might not sin against God." Psalm 119:105

"His Divine Power has given us everything we need for Life and Godliness through our knowledge of Him who called us by His own Glory and Goodness." 2 Peter 1:3

"Do not be conformed to this world, but be transformed by the renewing of your mind, so that you may prove what the Will of God is, that which is Good and Acceptable and Perfect." Romans 12:2

Every passage of Scripture that Bill Gothard used penetrated my heart. Jim too was very touched! Bill Gothard's presentation was so motivating. The Holy Spirit was working in our hearts! It seemed as though the Lord was preparing us for our life ahead. Our children were just babies and we needed to draw on the Truth of God's Word to equip us, and the Lord was providing.

"See to it that no one come short of the Grace of God; that no root of bitterness, springing up causes trouble, and by it many be defiled." Hebrews 12:15

The longer Bill Gothard talked and the more Scriptures he used, the more I wanted! I didn't want it to end! After the conference and in the following days and weeks, I started reading the Living Bible, underlining passages and writing notes in the margin. Then I went to the NIV, the New International Version doing the same thing and also memorizing passages. I couldn't believe that there was so much in the Bible that related to my personal life! This understanding changed my life. As long as I had been a believer in Christ, I had never taken the time to read God's Word daily, or to study it. Now, that's all I wanted to do! I felt different, also. There was an energy that excited me to know Him, from His Word.

"Blessed is the man who Trusts in the Lord. Whose confidence is in Him. He will be like the tree that is planted by the water, that sends out its roots by the stream. It has no worries in a year of drought. It never fails to bear fruit!" Jeremiah 17:8

"Thank You, Lord for once again using the Body of Christ (Betty) to direct me toward You! Lord, I want to be like that tree that is planted by the water that sends out its roots by the stream...I want to always bear fruit in response to Your Love for me."

The Dream

I looked forward to reading the Scriptures each evening and also talking to the Lord and bringing before Him my praise, thanksgiving, supplications and requests. I wanted a relationship with Him like never before. One night during one of my routine quiet times, I became aware of how much I wanted to be pleasing to the Lord; to live in such way that would please Him. I began to sob as I pleaded with Him to make me a blessing to Him. I realized that to be pleasing to Him, I must become holy as He is Holy. I certainly knew that I was not like Him in complete holiness. I knew that Christ had made me completely holy (positionally) because of His death on the cross, His resurrection and my faith in Him but I also knew that it was my responsibility to respond with a life totally committed to Him.

2 Timothy 1:9 states, "The God Who has saved us and called us to a holy life – not because of anything we have done but because of His own Purposes and Grace. This Grace was given us in Christ Jesus before the beginning of time."

I began to sob again and plead with Him to fill me completely and make me like His Son. I wanted to have nothing in me but Him! As I sat on my knees next to my bed before God in the quiet of the night, my heart finally settled, and I got up and went to bed. During the night, I had a dream. I dreamed that I was in complete and total darkness except for a tiny little light like a pinhole off in the far distance. I kept looking at the tiny light and noticed that it was getting closer and closer, brighter and bigger! And as it did, I noticed that it was filling me proportionally to its increasing size and brilliance! The light kept coming and it was continuing to fill me powerfully with its extraordinary luminescence. It was so pure and white! It kept coming and filling. I couldn't handle it! It was too much, and it scared me. I wanted it to stop! And just at that moment, I awoke with an abrupt start! With my eyes wide open, I sat up in bed, breathless. The room was quiet and dark, and I realized that I had had a dream. It was so real.

Then I remembered the struggle I had before going to bed. I slid down into the covers thinking about what had just happened and what I had asked of the Lord before I went to bed. I realized that through the dream, the Lord had answered my pleading heart! God is going to make me like His Son. But it will be a little at a time. He has predetermined that!

"For those God Foreknew He also Predestined to be Conformed to the Likeness of His Son that He might be the firstborn among many brothers." Romans 8:29

I am going to be holy through the sanctifying work of the Holy Spirit, a little at a time as God chooses to reveal Himself. His timing is perfect. It is going to be a progressive revelation and Work of God. He will be working in my daily life, through His Word and my obedience to it, and all the time God already sees the Righteousness of Christ covering me. His Sanctifying Work on the Cross has already paid the penalty for my unholy acts. I also realized from the dream that God is so much Greater than I am and so "Other."

"For My Thoughts are not your thoughts neither are your ways My Ways, declares the Lord. As the heavens are higher than the earth so are My Ways higher than your ways and My Thoughts than your thoughts." Isaiah 55:8,9

There is no way in my flesh, that I can possibly contain with complete understanding all that God is. He would be so Fearsome, so Huge, so Imposing, so Majestic, so Pure, so Holy, I would explode; as the light pictured in my dream became so intense and so penetratingly bright that I could not continue even looking at it! When I stand before God in glory someday, with my imperishable, glorified body, I will know Him as I am known, and I will see Him face-to-face.

"For we know in part and we prophesy in part, but when perfection comes, the imperfect disappears." I Corinthians 13:9-12

Until then I must go through this life's experiences a step at a time, taking each trial, each joy, as a means through which the Lord causes me to become pleasing to Him, as is His Son.

"For those God Foreknew, He also Predestined to be Conformed to the Likeness of His Son." Romans 8:29

Thank You, Lord so much, for speaking to my heart and giving me such security in You. Thank You for giving me a glimpse, through a powerful dream, of what Your Word had already revealed concerning Your Unapproachable Light! Wow!

"Keep the commandment without stain or reproach until the appearing of our Lord Jesus Christ which He will bring about at the proper time - He who is the Blessed and Only Sovereign, the King of kings and Lord of lords, Who alone Possesses Immortality and dwells in Unapproachable Light, Whom no man has seen or can see. To Him be Honor and Eternal Dominion! Amen." I Timothy 6:14-16

"No one has seen God at any time; the Only Begotten God Who is in the bosom of the Father, has explained Him." John 1:18

"Oh, the depth of the riches of the Wisdom and Knowledge of God! How Unsearchable His Judgments and His Paths beyond tracking out! Who has known the mind of the Lord? Or who has been His counselor? Who has ever given to God, that God should repay Him? For from Him and through Him and to Him are all things. To Him be the glory forever! Amen." Romans 11:33-36

Meanwhile, as Jim and I continued to serve in the church, and our church kept growing, our pastor and the church began to realize that we needed an expository pastor; one who taught the Scriptures, line upon line. This type of teaching contrasted to the present pastor's gift of evangelism, that focused on the need for an individual to accept Jesus as his personal Savior. An expository teacher focuses on new believers who need to grow and mature through the study of God's Word. This contrasted with the present pastor's gift of evangelism. As a result, our pastor answered the call to another ministry and we found ourselves needing a new pastor. A pulpit committee was formed to find him.

The Prayer

Because Jim had proven himself so trustworthy in other areas in the business of the church, he was asked to be the chairman of the Pulpit Committee. This meant that the Pulpit Committee would invite selected pastors who were gifted in the area of expository teaching to become a candidate. A weekend would be arranged and the candidate would be invited as a house guest of one of the church families. They then would deliver the message Sunday morning. This would give the candidate, as well as the church, an opportunity to meet one another. There was only one difficulty. There were no volunteers to house the pastors when arrangements needed to be made. We had an extra bedroom downstairs with a private bath. I was a stay-at- home mom, and I welcomed the idea of having the candidates stay with us anytime there was a need.

It took much longer to find the man God had chosen for our church than we thought, so there were many candidates that passed through. But these men were servants of the Living God, and I was so impressed with each one! They were so humble, grateful, and kind. Their desires were to be where the Lord wanted them to be. They spoke lovingly of their families. They were also interested in us and wanted to know how they could pray for us.

As time went on I grew more and more affected by their presence in our home. They all were so delightful, I would have had any one of them for my pastor! Sometimes after they would leave I would fall on my knees and with deep emotion thank the Lord for allowing me the privilege to serve them. I would find myself in tears, when I began to think how wonderful it would it be to serve them and their families, in a restful, quiet, private place. "Maybe," I said to myself, "the Lord would allow me to serve pastors and their families, this way, after our children are raised." I began to pray for the opportunity someday. When I would have my prayer time, I would look forward to including prayer for this privilege. It was like an obsession, or a compulsion. I felt drawn by something beyond me to pray for this.

This was certainly unusual so as I thought about it I believed that it was the Lord who was laying all of these things on my heart. It was so delightful to pray for what it might look like. Maybe there could be a pond with ducks; something peaceful, with water. Maybe there would be a long, winding driveway that would lead to a beautiful, secluded, quiet place. I could hardly wait to come before the Lord with these thoughts. I began to pray for where this place might be located. I felt that pastors would relax best in a place where creation is seen in solitude, and time with God could be available without interruption. Even Jesus withdrew by Himself into the hills, I thought.

"Jesus knowing that they intended to come and take Him by force as King, withdrew again into the hills by Himself." John 6:15
"At daybreak Jesus went out to a solitary place." Luke 4:42
"After leaving them, He went into the hills to pray." Mark 6:46
"After He had dismissed them, He went up into the hills by Himself to pray. When evening came He was there alone." Matthew 14:23

As all these thoughts ran through my mind I thought about the unlikeliness of these things becoming reality. Jim, was an Industrial Engineer, how would these things fit with him? He has supported us so faithfully and so well. To be employed, he needs to be in a large city. So was I asking for something unlikely? Yes, but I just knew that the Lord would work that out too. Nothing is Impossible for Him! And

I continued to ask the Lord for, "Just a piece of His Beautiful Creation, so that the pastor's minds could fall on Him and what He has made known about Himself through all He has Created."

You have told us in Your Word that, in the things You have Made, Your Invisible Qualities, Your Eternal Power, and Divine Nature; You have told us that in These Things, You are clearly seen.

"Since what may be known about God is plain to them because God has made it plain to them for since the creation of the world God's Invisible Qualities, His Eternal Power and Divine Nature have been clearly seen being understood from what has been made, so that men are without excuse." Romans 1:19-20

What a restful and restoring balm all these things would be for a weary servant of God!

I also asked that the pastors could receive this without charge. I felt it would spoil everything if we had to ask for a fee...so I asked for provision to support this ministry. I didn't know where this would come from, but I felt sure that the Lord would provide. In fact, I really didn't know how any of these prayers would become a reality. We were happily planted in California, enjoying all we had been given there. But what did I know? I knew that I was driven by an excited, happy, delightful energy to pray. And during those prayer times, the Lord would add things as the weeks, months and years went on, even to the sheets I would put on the bed, and the pillow cases that Jim's grandmothers had hand-crocheted. Being an only child, my mother had saved silverware, beautiful dish sets, linens and other lovely things she thought I would like someday. When I thought of these things, I saw them used for the pastors. I wanted the pastors to have the best of what we had to offer. It was like I was serving Jesus Himself. These were some of the requests that I made before the Father on behalf of His precious servants.

Colorado Or Washington State?

Our children were approaching school age, and our sweet time we had with them at home as babies was coming to an end. I knew that sending them out into the world exposed them to the "prince and power of the air" but at this time there were no other alternatives. I would depend on the Lord to put His shield about them.

It was about this time that Jim came home one day from work with surprising news. He had been successful in the corporate world. When he was at Rockwell, he was even offered a plant manager's position in California, but Jim always put our family before his career. Now Rockwell was offering him an opportunity to accept a position either located in Washington State or Colorado!

He asked me, "Missie, (his pet name for me) which one do you want? Both are great opportunities for my career, so you call it! Just let me know!" I was elated! I had been praying about the location of this pastor's retreat for a couple years. I had felt that it wasn't California in our present home because it seemed too busy and people were everywhere! Open land was not plentiful.

Both Washington State and Colorado had beautiful rural areas! Wow! Was the Lord working out my prayer? But I believed that as long as we were in the throes of raising our children it would not be wise to divide our attention. So I began to fervently ask the Lord to give me an answer concerning the location. Maybe one of these places was it!

"Lord," I requested. "Jim wants me to give him an answer. Would You please tell me what You want for this pastor's retreat? I only want what You want. Lord, You know when he needs to tell Rockwell, so I'm trusting that You will let us know in just the right timing. Your timing is always best."

Silence. Nothing. I didn't receive anything! Time was going by and Jim would ask me, "Can you tell me what you are thinking? What place should we pursue?" I had nothing to tell him. I truly did not know.

Then when it had been approaching two weeks since Jim had told me of this opportunity, I was walking by the night stand by our bed. I looked down to see the back of a magazine with a large beautiful picture of a waterfall. The water was splashing down a craggy, rocky slope, spraying as it bounced along with white and sparkly droplets. Evergreens lined each side of the dancing water. It was like the picture was alive! It was beautiful! I said to the Lord, "That's it, Lord! That's the place I picture for the pastor's retreat; a place that has natural spots *Just Like That*!" As I was taking all of this in, my eyes dropped down to the corner of the picture and there were the words, "Coors Beer, Golden, Colorado!" There it was! My answer! I was so sure that the Lord had led me to this! "Thank You, Lord! Colorado it is!" I shared my revelation with Jim when he came home and plans were made to move! Our beautiful home sold quickly. In the 10 years we lived there, its value tripled. We had paid $37,000 and it sold for $110,000.

"Thank You, Lord. We now have sufficient funds to have a home in Colorado. Our Blessings overflow!"

Rocky Flats Golden, Colorado

In a large, impressive, sprawling building, set in the middle of a field of hundreds of open acres, dry and rocky, desert-like, was the environment surrounding the grounds and place where Jim would be employed. So, disappeared was the belief that Jim, as an Industrial Engineer, could only be supported by industry within a large city. There was absolutely no city here! The facility where Jim became employed was in this remote, desolate area, and evidence of the Lord continued to demonstrate His Guiding Presence. The information on the magazine on our night stand indicated Golden, Colorado. The plant where Jim became employed was in Golden, Colorado! How specific is God's answer and direction!

"Praise You, Lord! You are so specific in Your answers and in Your direction. How Miraculous are Your Ways!"

Delberts

Strutting peacocks with tails spread open were pridefully displaying iridescent colors of indigo, violet, gold and yellow. They stepped gingerly around in spacious cages. Furry, domesticated bunnies of all colors were hopping every which way, freely and unafraid. A small pond, which had been known to have had ducks, glistened in the sun. The terrain on this 40-acre property was perfectly flat except for a down-sloping incline toward a pond. A small, neat two-bedroom house was set on the incline and overlooked the pond. There were no other houses around. The nearest neighbor was too far away to even greet with a wave. No other buildings were there except an old pile of wood, hardly recognizable as a "used-to-be-barn." The terrain was dry and rocky all the way to Jim's work facility, about a 20-minute drive (no wonder his work place became known as "Rocky Flats").

The house had been the home of Delbert, and his wife of many years. I'm certain the house and the property held many happy memories of a lifetime gone by. His wife having passed away recently, Delbert now wanted to rent out his home. Because we needed a temporary place to live until we found a home, here we stood looking at the possibility of becoming Delbert's renters. There really was no need to debate. Our answer had already been made for us. We were just stepping into what our Loving Lord had already planned for us. After all, what was the address of this little house? The address was Golden, Colorado! Just as had been shown to me on the magazine!

"Dear Lord, once again You demonstrate Your Presence in our lives and guide us so clearly! Thank You! You never make mistakes!"

There was something very special and peaceful about Delbert's home. It was quite a contrast to the busyness of California! The children (now seven and five) loved it. Also, they were just the right ages to really enjoy the animals. Kim had always loved horses, so we bought a pony from a man down the road. The children anticipated another fun experience. They looked forward to sleeping in the same room together in bunk beds! Our bedroom was so close to theirs, at night we could all hear each other breathing. That was, somehow, very pleasant and reassuring for the children. School was not to begin for about a month, so we all enjoyed the summer days in this wonderful place. Even after the children grew to adulthood, when asked what some of their best memories from childhood were, they always said, "Delbert's."

Soda Creek, In Evergreen

Fall came, school started, the children were settled in school and the hot summer days moved into warm days and brisk nights. Having lived in California for the past 10 years I had become less discerning of the change in the seasons. Delbert explained this was called "Indian Summer" and about this time every year in the Colorado Rocky Mountains this beautiful transition into winter is displayed. The brilliant gold of the aspen and deep hues of the evergreens come together on a backdrop of an azure, cloudless sky. With these colors climbing dramatically up the slopes of the majestic Rocky Mountains, which were sometimes snowcapped, people traveled miles just to take in the magnificent attraction. It's one of the things that makes Colorado one of the most beautiful places in America.

I had been out with our realtor, Kathy, almost every day for the past few weeks wanting to purchase a property with a few acres. She took me everywhere within the perimeter of reason but there was absolutely nothing available! Even though it looked like Colorado had vast acres of open land which to purchase, that's just all it was, hundreds of acres of vast land but nothing subdivided. Pre-existing homes were very close together and if they were on 3 or 4 acres, to allow horses, all were cramped together. Ranches (and we weren't ranchers) were further away from Jim's work and the drive for Jim would be unreasonable. And to become ranchers would be unreasonable! Kathy had mentioned a place called, "Evergreen."

It would be about a 45-minute drive to work each day for Jim so I had dismissed it as an option. But now, seeing that there was nothing within reasonable distance in the immediate area, I asked Kathy to show me Evergreen.

As we drove up I-70, I could see that we were getting in a higher elevation. We were leaving the Denver flat land and moving up to the mountains. There were rolling hills and evergreens, and aspen changing color. Soon we came to a sign saying, "Soda Creek, Next Exit." I was very interested. The travel time seem like nothing. There were no traffic lights!

Soda Creek in Evergreen was a newly subdivided area just off I-70. It had been a 1,000-plus acre cattle ranch but was subdivided into parcels no less than five acres. The size of each parcel varied. Some were 14 acres, some 25, some 10, and any number in between. It depended on the lay of the land. The first filing had been completely sold out and many had already built their impressive, custom homes. It was beautiful just driving around on the gently curving road, with mansion-like houses set back among aspen and pines.

There were association fee requirements and building restrictions so that there was a standard set in place for quality and appropriate architecture. Thesecond filing had just opened, and we could have our choice from many available parcels. When I shared all of this with Jim he was anxious to see so we wasted no time in driving up to the area. We felt that we had found the right spot! Yes we would need to build, but we were in a good holding place at Delbert's in Golden. We were also encouraged to know that we could build a modest home, and because most of the rest of the houses were more expensive, our modest home would carry more value if we ever sold it.

The piece of ground that caught our eye was five acres, about five minutes from the I-70 entrance (handy for Jim's commute). The house site was up on a mountain side overlooking almost all of the entire five acre meadow below (a great place for Kim's pony, "Happy"). Compared to California, this area looked huge! Looking at Jim and the children, running around in the meadow from the building site, they looked a few inches tall! Jim and I both were excited about building a house and coming to live here. Our plans to build became a reality.

Ever since the Lord so specifically directed us to this location through the magazine on the night table, I continued to pray. I knew for

sure that all of what happened was a part of God's answer to my prayer. However, I felt in my heart that this home that we were to build in Evergreen was not the one for the pastor's retreat.

First, our home on five acres which was more than enough for us, could be confining for anyone who wanted to go on a mile hike in the woods. With other homes here, although far apart, there was more activity on the street. It would be harder to find solitude. I felt there was more coming; much more that the Lord would provide for His Beloved Pastors. I must be about caring for our family and be willing to wait on the Lord's Timing. Our children were only ages 6 and 8.

School Days, School Days

Moving into a newly constructed house is always a treat! Everything smells so good! The new wood on the floor, the freshly painted items, even the wallpaper had its own new smell. Kim had her pony, "Happy." Kevin had a little Mongoose bike and plenty of room to ride. But school was going to be starting soon and I had a few concerns.

Kim and Kevin had attended school in Golden the previous year while living at Delbert's. The school had suggested Kevin be tested. We gave them permission and the results showed that Kevin had a high IQ and language skills of a 10-year-old, but his hyperactivity and a learning disability could hinder his progress; especially in reading. They believed he would need to have extra help and learn differently. Because we would be in a new school and not returning to Golden, I thought I would wait until we got to Evergreen to follow up on this information. Maybe we would need to send Kevin to a Christian school. Jim and I wanted the best for our little boy. School could be miserable for him and being just six years old, he had a long way to go. I decided to ask the Lord to pave the way for Kevin.

"Would You please Lord, provide a Christian principal, and teachers that will be patient and be able to teach him to read? I pray that we will not need to search for a Christian school, because the principal is a Christian and you have chosen just the right teachers to be available. Thank You Lord for hearing my prayer."

Bergen Elementary was the name of the neighborhood school in Jefferson County, only five minutes from our house, so I set up a time to meet with the principal. His name was Jerry Williams, and the more we talked, the more I began to believe he was a Christian! And indeed, he was! He and his family attended Conference Baptist Church (where we had also decided to attend). He even had a daughter Kim's age. His school was the central location for Special Education and special needs children. Kevin's teacher, Mrs. Peyton, was a remedial reading specialist as well as special needs teacher. She had an excellent reputation and she would teach Kevin one-on-one!

"What answers to prayer, Lord! Thank You, Thank You! I have complete confidence in where You have led us."

When Kevin had finished the fifth grade, the principal Jerry Williams, made an appointment to see me. He believed that we would need to be thinking of alternatives to middle school, so that the good work for Kevin could continue. I had been listening to the radio broadcast of James Dobson, a renown Christian Psychiatrist. He had several programs on home school. This was a very new concept and it caught my attention. I wanted to know more so I wrote a letter to Dr. Dobson explaining our situation. He responded with a strong encouragement to home-school. When I shared this with Mr. Williams, with the question, "What do you think?" he responded with, "I don't know! It's never been done in Evergreen before!"

Kevin and I were the first to home-school in Evergreen. We began in the sixth grade and continued until we enrolled him in a Christian school for his Junior and Senior years of high school. I asked the Lord to help him earn straight A's his Senior year. I wanted him to see that he could get A's from objective teachers, not just from his mom. On his final report card, he got straight A's! We were so proud of him! And you should have heard him read!

"Thank You, again Lord! You continue to place Your Loving Hand on every aspect of our lives! Miracles, Miracles!"

Answers Begin

The years had flown by and here I was sitting at our kitchen table listening to the bubbling of what I called," Hamburger Hooper" (my special twist to spice up hamburger). Dinner was ready, and I was

just sitting on a kitchen stool waiting for Jim to come in from work. As I sat there, I began contemplating Kim going away to Wheaton College in Wheaton, Illinois. She had done very well academically in high school, graduating with honors, and we were happy for her to be going to such a fine Christian school. I had told her not to worry about the cost because I would go back to teaching until she finished.

Kevin had gone to Camp Tadmor, a Christian camp in Oregon for the summer and would be finishing up his Senior year in high school starting in the Fall of 1987. He wanted to pursue Emergency Medical Training. "Our children are growing up", I thought. At this point, I heard Jim coming in from work. I served my Hamburger Hooper and we sat down to eat, then said our routine thanksgiving dinner blessing, like we had done more than 100 times before.

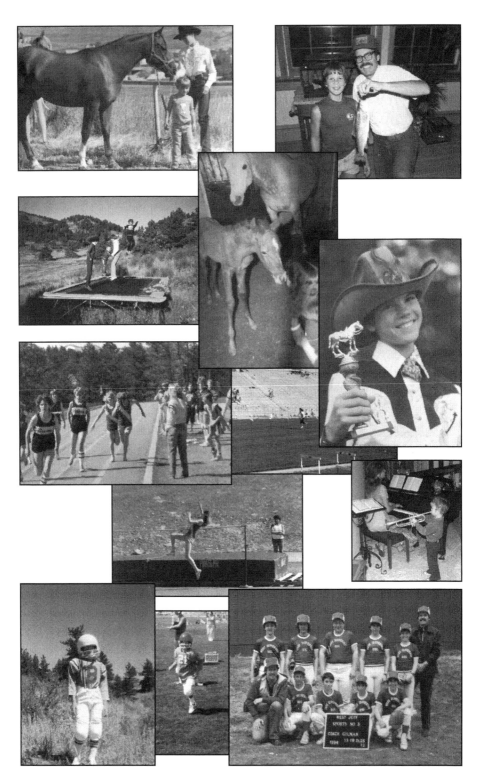

The Lord had been so faithful. One hundred more times of saying, "Thank You" would not have been adequate to express my thanks to Him. Our lives raising our children in Colorado these past 10 years now were becoming sweet memories. Changes were about to come.

Upon finishing our meal, Jim lingered at the table. He said without any hesitation in his voice, "I'm quitting the corporate world! I've been in it for 30 years and I've had enough!" I had grown accustomed to hearing these powerful life changing proclamations through the years. But this time I had a feeling that the prayers that I had been holding in my heart concerning the pastor's retreat may now be in God's timing. Our children were on the brink of young adulthood and I had a sense of anticipation and excitement.

"Oh Lord," I called to Him. "For almost 15 years I have had this prayer on my heart. Is this Your Timing for us to watch You do, 'Exceeding, Abundantly beyond all that we could ask or think?' May You alone be Praised!" Ephesians 3:20

Land For Sale?!

The horseshoes clanged against the metal posts as the men either cheered for a ringer or groaned as their horseshoe thudded in the sand. We were, "The Horseshoe Gang" a small group of couples from Conference Baptist who enjoyed coming to Paul Bilby's annual "Horse Shoe Gang BBQ." Paul, a very sweet elderly gentleman and his wife, Peggy, are the ones who named us and organized these fun outings. They lived on a 40-acre ranch and it was always a treat to enjoy not only the lovely people, but their property. Their property was further out where larger portions of land lined the winding roads. During the ten years of attending Conference Baptist Church, if any one knew me well, they had heard about my desire to have a pastor's retreat and my commitment to pray. I had shared my desire and my compelling obsession to pray the details of it with many precious Christian friends.

When our BBQ was over, Jim suggested something that he had never suggested before. "Let's drive up the road and see if there is

any land for sale." Was I hearing correctly? All the time I have prayed for this pastor's retreat, I never wanted Jim to think that he had to do something to fulfill the answer to my prayers. We had never discussed plans as to how to make this prayer happen. This was between God and me and I knew if God wanted Jim to be involved, He knew how to speak to him. Now we were not restrained to the commute to Rocky Flats. Jim's decision to leave the corporate world left options for us that had not been present before. Since that decision, he had been doing some Industrial Engineering consulting, but he was really looking forward to trying real estate. He had started working on his real estate license. Was the Lord's Time Clock putting all these things together? Might I see today the place the Lord has determined for the pastor's retreat? God was leading, this I knew. Sometimes when it was God's Timing things moved very quickly!

On our way up the road we came to a real estate office and decided to stop in. We asked if there were any parcels of land in the area for sale and the lady said, "Oh, yes, there are some large parcels just up Highway 285 past the town of Bailey, in Shawnee." She gave us directions and we were off! When we arrived the real estate agent who had listed the land, Rich Johnson, was there looking at maps spread out on the hood of his car. He was attempting to determine the property lines. When he realized we had some questions and were directed to the land by the real estate office, he gave us details. He explained that it was a 450-acre parcel with a modest home on it and the North Fork of the South Platte River ran through it. Highway 285 divided it. Jim and I were really struck with the uniqueness of the river and its rugged beauty, however we certainly were not interested in that much land and having the property split with the highway was not a plus for us, either. Watching cars buzz by was not my idea of a peaceful setting. "No." I said to myself. "The river was special but this was not the land." There were too many hesitations. We asked Rich if he knew of any smaller property for sale along the river. He didn't know of any. We thanked him for his help and got in the car to process all we had seen. This was August of 1987.

Rich Johnson knew that we were interested in purchasing a smaller parcel, so as he sold parcels of the 450-acre property he had listed, he would call and tell us that we had better hurry up and make an offer on some of it, because it was going fast. The busyness of the road going through the middle of the land just didn't set with the peace and tranquility we pictured.

Kim came home in October; the weekend of the Wheaton Home-coming and we were excited to include her in our pursuit. We took her out to see the property on a cold, windy October day. The wind and the cold didn't deter her from loving the river and all the open meadows, but by January of 1988, all that large parcel was sold piece by piece. The thought ran through my mind, "Would there ever be an opportunity like that again?" I didn't care about that at all!

The Lord would lead us to what He wanted, river or no river. There will be no hesitations. Jim and I will both know in agreement. I remembered that I had asked in my prayer for a pond with ducks or some peaceful water setting. Now here was a rushing river. But all of this was to be His plan and what He wanted.

In January of 1988, after all that land was sold, Jim suggested that we walk along the river and when we see a house, stop and ask the residents if they know of someone want-ing to sell their property.

This we did, and we came to a man who was very helpful. He told us that he didn't know the status of the land now, but the owner's name was David Ray. Mr. Ray had been trying, for a long time to sell his property without an agent, so he had been putting large signs along the road, but he had no one interested. He finally gave up and took the signs down. He also had been asking an exorbitant amount of money for the land. The gentleman who was sharing this information told us that the land was next door to the North Fork Guest Ranch. We thanked him and determined to locate David Ray. Within the hour we were knocking on his door!

A Salty Character

We knocked on the door when suddenly it flew open and an elderly man, David Ray, stood in front of us. He looked to be in his late 60's and we discovered that he was a salty old guy with quite a reputation. We explained that one of his neighbors had told us that he had had a parcel of land along the river for sale, and that we were interested in seeing it if it were still available. At that point he interrupted, cursed loudly and shouted, "I just put it on the market with a real estate agent yesterday! No one has even seen it, neither has the agent and there isn't even a sign on it!"

There we were, standing before him, led by the Hand of God, to the land that we now know was the "piece of God's beauty" I had asked for in my prayer. The Lord had been preparing and protecting it for us. Now, the Lord had led us to a man, whom He prepared, eager to sell, frustrated with his solo attempts, and willing to take the counsel of a real estate agent who would advise him of a reasonable price.

"Lord, Your Presence in the Past, Present and Future is seen so vividly! Thank You for letting us be swept up in Your Perfect Timing!"

"If I rise on the wings of the dawn, if I settle on the far side of the sea, even there Your Hand will Guide me. Your Right Hand will Hold me fast." Psalm 139: 9,10

GILMAN RANCH, COLORADO 2014

A Piece Of God's Beauty!

The entrance to David Ray's 36-acre property was off Highway 285 on a narrow, dirt driveway. A high incline was to the right and a 50-foot drop-off down into the roaring river, was to the left. As we drove in, and I looked down over the opened car window, down over the 50-foot drop, the river was wild and loud and untamed! A wave of fear gripped me. The ride was slow and bumpy. David Ray drove carefully, explaining that there was another entrance through the North Fork Ranch, that is the one typically used, but he wanted us to see that there was a direct entrance from Highway 285. This was my first introduction to David Ray's property. It was dramatic, breathtaking, roaring and loud and a bit frightening, but glorious!

Coming down on the primitive driveway led us into a valley and turned us around into a beautiful meadow. We were now facing the river off in the distance, no longer below us. Even though we were in the valley, the lay of the land was gently rolling and it had an interesting terrain. As we continued to drive back into the property, we followed this gently curving driveway through a long corridor of aspen and willows. Then we were led across an old broken-down bridge. The water rushed by with a sparkling purity and the sound of it was musical. It rapidly flowed by, seeming to dance playfully along. We were informed that the property had an entire half-mile of river frontage, and that the neighbors on each side of us stocked it regularly with trout! Having crossed the river, we entered another beautiful meadow that was lush in growth because the river constantly watered it. The aspen and willows lining the driveway gave the area a secluded feel. Coming through them, on the left, there was a grove of aspen in the middle of the meadow. We continued past the meadow and we were led to a large plateau above the river. It was dug into a hillside and was perfectly flat. David Ray told us that the water board years ago, had dug rocks out of this mountain side to line the river; but it was a perfect house site! It not only overlooked the river meandering through the property, but also showcased a spectacular panoramic view of the mountain range with Shawnee Peak being the tallest at 12,000 feet.

The scene was beautiful! Sometimes, we were told Shawnee Peak would be snow-capped and sparkle in the sun against a deep blue Colorado sky and nothing was prettier. Also, there were no houses or roof tops to distract from the view. Everything looked pristine, like it had never been touched. We were told that no other area of the Rockies has such a diversity of wildlife. Elk, deer, bighorn sheep, mountain goats, bear, mountain lions, and beaver could be found in this area. I could see beautiful trails and lovely spots for quiet meditation. There were short walks with many stops for reflection.

In my prayer, I remember asking the Lord for "a piece of His creative beauty." I began to see how He had answered my prayer absolutely, and why the Lord led us to Colorado! I see now why so many people want to live in this state. The Creative Work of the Lord's Hand is in every season and every mountainous scene with spectacular display!

"Thank You, Lord. Wow! May many who use the pastor's retreat be Blessed by the voice of Your Creation which declares all of Your Invisible Attributes!"

Walking around the house site, there was a trail. It led out about 500 feet then turned into Pike National Forest, 13,000 acres of wilderness. This National Forest adjoined David Ray's property and there was no public access through David Ray's private property. That would mean that no one could go through this private property unless the owners would give permission. And that would be us! It was truly a solitary place. I remember asking the Lord for a private place for the pastors and their families to hike and be in God's creation without the distraction of the public. "Lord! You did it again! Praise Your Name!" Jim and I both agreed that this was the Lord's Hand in Leading us to such a place! This was January of 1988 and we wholeheartedly paid the asking price for the 36 acres (11 acres on one side of the river and 25 acres on the other). The closing date was in March of 1988. The next step was to sell our Soda Creek home.

Aunt Dell And Uncle Jack

The market had been depressed and high-end homes were not selling. Some homes in Soda Creek had been on the market for years! If they did sell they had been on the market for a long time. Jim asked me how much we should ask, and I said that we needed to ask a price that gives room "to wiggle." If we received $330,000 that would be a blessing. Therefore, an asking price of $359,000 would give us some room to negotiate. Jim said that was exactly the price he had determined also. Was this a coincidence? "Not at all!" I said to myself. "The Lord was moving!" When I heard this, I knew the Lord was letting me know that He was Present. We felt that it might take as long as a year to sell, so Jim, now a realtor, decided to list it. However, he had not yet advertised it, put up a sign, or put it in the MLS!

In the meantime we learned that Jim's Aunt Dell and Uncle Jack were coming from Michigan to visit. We wanted everything to be in place, so Jim and I really went to work. On a particularly nice spring day, Jim planted and raked and mowed until it looked like a professional gardener had come. He even mowed the meadows where the horses graze so that it looked like the Kentucky Bluegrass! I went to work on the inside of the house: polishing, cleaning, vacuuming and putting everything in place and the stage was set! It looked like those California model homes we had been smitten by years ago. We were ready for Jack and Dell! But the Lord had someone else to impress. These things were in His Timing and His Plans would not be thwarted.

On this very day, barely finishing up our work, there was a knock on our front door. It was a realtor named Reggie, and with him was an interested party. Reggie had met Jim during his real estate classes and had learned that Jim was going to put our house on the market. Reggie wondered if he could show our home to him. We were very pleasantly surprised! The property was ready to show, thanks to Aunt Dell's anticipated visit and God's Perfect Timing!

They walked through the house in silence. When they were finished, they happened to be outside near a wooden swing hanging from our porch. It overlooked the meadow. The flowers and the spring green colors were fresh and fragrant; the scene from the swing was beautiful and pastoral. I had made some lemonade and invited them to sit and drink a glass. They sat there in the swing for quite a long time while the horses grazed peacefully below in the meadow. I could tell they were enjoying the reprieve and everything they saw. The scene slowed their pace to just take in the loveliness of the moment.

Later that very same day, Reggie gave us a call and told us that the gentleman he had brought to see our home wanted to make an offer. This completely surprised us! We believed that it was going to take months or maybe even years to sell it and now this was just after we had discussed the asking price. When the offer came to us, and the gentleman saw the $359,000 asking price, he made an offer of $330,000! Of course, we accepted the offer! It was the exact price on which Jim and I had agreed! Once again our Precious Lord revealed His Presence! The Lord had prompted us to prepare everything for Jack and Dell, but it had been prepared for God's purposes in continuing to answer my prayer. Things were moving so quickly! That next step, selling our Soda Creek home, was done!

Homeless!

The Soda Creek property was going to close in July of 1988 and that certainly was not enough time to find an architect, draw up special plans to accommodate a pastor's retreat and build it. It was obvious that we would need to rent somewhere until the Shawnee property and the pastor's retreat was completely finished. Until then where could we go? We had a house full of furniture and three horses!

Jim was now in real estate and had access to information concerning houses that come on the market. One in particular that came to Jim's attention was owned by Tom Brookshire, a popular sportscaster, who had been trying to sell his high-end Evergreen property for over a year. At this time, he lived in another state. This was an impressive estate with horse stables, grazing meadow, tennis courts, four bedrooms, a large living room, a family room, a kitchen, several baths, and it was furnished! All of this was set back off a long driveway leading into a forested backdrop. Jim saw this as an opportunity to ask Mr. Brookshire if we could rent his Evergreen property. His first answer was an absolute "No." Jim explained the advantage of receiving rent money, rather than letting it sit idly, and that he would consent to keeping it on the market, allowing people to come through for showings, and that he would also be responsible for any damage. Mr. Brookshire finally saw that it was to his advantage to rent it to us. The monthly rent was very reasonable. The Lord had granted us favor with Mr. Brookshire.

We had all our furnishings put in storage. I must confess that the thought occurred to me that the house might sell before we were ready to leave. I heard that wicked voice of temptation telling me not to try to sell the house; to not be too accommodating. I stopped! I couldn't believe that these thoughts were going through my mind! God had been so Good to me! How could that wicked thought be entertained at all? I determined right then that I would treat the house and the effort to sell it as my own. If a showing were planned, I would "set the stage" and make it as homey and as attractive as I could. I was true to my word. Everything I could do to present the house at its very best, I did. Showings came and went. The Lord honored my repentance and commitment. We lived in comfort until August of 1989 and it sold one week after we moved out!

"Dear Lord, there is once again evidence of Your Presence in our lives! Psalm 97:12 states, "You who are Godly, be glad because of what the Lord has done. Praise Him, because He is Holy!"

Mel Birkey, A Gracious Friend

During the time we lived at Brookshire's, we drew up preliminary plans for the pastor's retreat. Our home in California was very open and bright and I wanted to duplicate the floor plan somewhat, but when I tried to put the roof on, I knew it was going to take a professional architect, and their fees were exorbitant! One architect after another would look at our sketched plans and then quote a price that we couldn't afford. Finally, a precious friend and architect from our church, Mel Birkey, offered to draw ours up free of charge! He was experienced and had drawn up plans for many large and unique projects. He was creative, talented and excellent in all he did. He came to the property with a camera, stood on the house site and took panoramic pictures of the view. Every window was a postcard picture of this beautiful spot the Lord had given. When all was said and done, I couldn't believe it! Tears came to my eyes as the plans were completed and I saw the reality of my prayer, as drawn from Mel's hand. I had asked the Lord for a structure so beautiful that upon driving across the bridge and looking up at the home our pastor guests would exclaim, "Wow! Look where we get to stay!" It was more impressive than I ever prayed!

The Well

We needed to have a well drilled on the Shawnee property. Water is a precious commodity. In the early West, people killed one another over the rights to water. Water is scarce here in Colorado and often dry wells are drilled. A home without water is a huge detriment to the property. Having many guests taking showers frequently would certainly tax a well and it might clearly not produce enough to support the usage. Having a well that pumped three gallons of water per minute would support a small household, but not very extravagantly. Knowing all this, I brought it before the Lord.

"Lord, would you please grant us an exceptional well? One that is a real gusher, like, sixty gallons a minute so that our guests will have plenty?" This was a huge request! Sixty gallons a minute would truly be like a fire hydrant!

October 14, 1988 was the day for the well to be drilled. This was very important. The guest ranch next door had struggled with water and they were lower in altitude and closer to the river's banks than we.

Later that day, the well driller called to report the results. I heard Jim answer the phone, so I ran to the phone hearing only Jim's side of the conversation. "Yes", Jim said, "You have finished drilling? And what? You have stopped counting at 60 gallons a minute? It's what? A real gusher?" The well driller used the exact same words that I had used in my prayer! The Lord overwhelmed me once again with the evidences of His Presence and His Good Pleasure in what we were doing!

I am reminded repeatedly of Jesus' Words when He says, "Which of you, if his son asks for bread, will give him a stone? Or if he asks for a fish, will give him a snake? If you then, though you are evil, know how to give good gifts to your children, how much more will your Father in heaven give good gifts to those who ask Him." Matthew 7:9-11

We Need A Barn! And House!

While we were renting at Brookshire's, it dawned on us that we needed to build a barn for our horses. We also thought that it would save rent money if we could put in an apartment instead of a hay loft above the barn. We could live there until our home would be completed. Electricity and water needed to be put in the barn for the horses anyway, so we believed that this would be a wise but simple and sensible use of the barn. Jim put in some wire fences around one of the meadows so that the horses could be taken care of as soon as we were ready to move into the barn. It was a pole barn, with two bedrooms, one that was able to accommodate a king-sized bed, the other to have a bunk bed. The living room was open with a high ceiling and shared this area with the kitchen. The couch in the living room opened into a queen-sized bed. We even had a stone fire place later. The barn was completed August of 1989 and we moved in. We would be able to watch the pastor's retreat plans drawn by Mel materialize before our eyes.

As Mel worked on the plans for the area for the pastors, I wanted the bedroom to really be special. A high vaulted ceiling, so it would have a special spacious feeling, a custom tile hot tub for 2 in the bathroom, pretty colors with a touch of Victorian floral. But most of all I wanted this bedroom to be in a prime location to display the river below, with windows that would take it all in. Our bedroom would be out of ear shot from the upstairs, so that there would be complete privacy.

The plans were finally finished and it was time to get bids from builders.

Every builder we spoke to gave bids far beyond what we could afford. $500,000 was consistent among the builders. We had already purchased the land, built the barn, and we certainly didn't have $500,000! One elderly man (Richard Jepsen) who had attended our church at one time, and who had spent a life time as a building contractor said that he would be willing to help Jim be the building contractor. He said that it would not cost anywhere near $500,000 if Jim would accept this responsibility. This would mean Jim would oversee the entire construction and hire various workmen to complete the various steps. Richard said that he knew the people in the area that would be good to hire.

Jim had experience building a small rental house while we lived in Evergreen and he knew what was involved, so with Richard's guidance he agreed to the idea.

A Trophy?

Richard got Jim started step by step. Jim was also getting more involved in real estate. More business kept coming to him until finally it became obvious that his time spent in real estate was making more money than he was saving trying to work on building the house. As the year progressed, more money kept coming in. He was even getting notoriety! The local newspaper wrote an article on Jim as being the "Million Dollar Salesman!" He was the top producer in all of Coldwell Banker throughout the Denver Metropolitan area, of which there were 400 agents! He kept earning more and more money! He was awarded "Rookie of the Year" with a huge trophy! With all of this we were able to pay for the land, the barn, and the building of the house! We even paid Mel Birkey who had generously and graciously drawn up those costly architectural plans free of charge. Jim has never made that much money since!

The Lord did this! I am learning that when the Lord wants something to be accomplished, He Enables it to happen with Miracles!

"The Lord is God, and He has made His Light Shine upon us. You are my God, and I will give You thanks; You are my God, and I will exalt You! Give thanks to the Lord, for He is Good; His Love Endures Forever!" Psalm 119:27-29

The Foreknowledge Of God

March 20, 1989 and we were still living at the Brookshire's Ranch, enjoying all that the Lord had led thus far. Soon, we would be leaving this lovely place of transition and all of us, horses included, would be moving into the little apartment over our barn. But right now this morning, I was continuing, as I had been doing each day, walking down the Brookshire's winding, sometimes snow-laced driveway to the barn to feed our horses. It was a particularly enchanting walk, this cold March morning. There was an ominous beauty in the sky, and what I saw brought me to a place of deep thought. It was at this time that I wrote what follows, never knowing what the Lord had in store.

Dawn begins so quietly, I thought – gently creeping over the mountainous horizon of the Colorado sky. Everything was so still and this morning the soft pink, coral horizon reflected its brilliance on the snow giving it a sparkling, rosy luminance. The stark black line of night, that marked the line of sunrise, seemed to remain a stubborn wall of obsidian, as if to cry at its passing and designation of time. I watched in silence, captured by the beauty.

My attention was drawn to the barn and the reason for my early rising. The horses moved anxiously in their stalls as they whinnied and acknowledged my approaching. Their muzzle whiskers, grown long from winter's cold were coated with glossy-white, glimmering needles and their warm breath was visible in frosty billows. Their ears perked to my every sound and motion. The sweet smell of molasses and grain rose to my senses when I removed the wooden lid of the old brown barrel. The soft scent of hay and alfalfa quickened my awareness of the pricking cold because I breathed deeply to savor its delicate aroma.

The Lord has been so good to me, I thought...so much to enjoy! My thoughts raced through my mind, attempting to collect all the joys and blessings in remembrance – so many that their abundance was just too much to contain. I sighed contentedly as I hoisted the bucket of grain to my side and began to fill the corner troughs. The horses stepped quickly to their breakfast with low deep whinnies and an eagerness that said, "thank you." I was grateful to be able to accommodate their needs and grateful that my own and those of my family are met so graciously; never to have known hunger or cold or homelessness or lack of love. Nothing stays the same and with the passing of time, can all be so sure for the future? The barn still dark, I sensed a foreboding gloom that hovered for an instant; an instant that compelled me to resist a new day - even dread a new day. Turning to the large, sliding barn door, with chores completed, I glided its massive bulk, with all the strength I had, to the right. With the quickness and force I had used to open the door, it unveiled a blast of morning sun. The brilliant rays of sun filled the barn with an exciting explosion! No longer was the night wall prevailing as I had noticed earlier. It had finally surrendered to the glory of the morning and the beginning of a new day. Time was passing, I thought, and with it was newness and bright hope.

Was I, at times, like that stubborn wall of obsidian that struck across the sky, blocking the approach of a new day with all its uncertainties? Was this a metaphor describing me? I thought of the Creator, who designed the days, who ordained time and the predictability of the sunrise. Was my life any less significant to Him than this seemingly mechanical phenomenon that was graced with such beauty and order? With the sun's warmth on my face and faith freshly flooding my soul, I greeted my new day with joy, hope, and exuberance!

I discovered this personal essay among my things in a drawer that had been unopened for a while. I had almost forgotten it. I wrote it for a continuing education class I had taken while living in Evergreen, at the Brookshire Ranch. I had no idea of the actual experiences that were to follow the writing of the essay. Truly those experiences were pictured by the black of night in this essay, never having been experienced before; a night that consumed me with unparalleled pain, anxiety, and grief lasting several years.

My father, diagnosed with cancer, died in October of 1989. I was diagnosed with cancer in 1990. These experiences sent me into dealing with death as I had never before. However, the years that followed were made up of a trusting and sweet dependency that changed my life forever. Those very black nights, I believe, were spoken of in this essay. I also believe these experiences have led to a fresh faith that now floods my soul, like the sun that bursts through the black night, also spoken of in the essay; a new day filled with joy, hope and exuberance. Our Lord is Faithful to use all things for our Good and His Glory, even in those times of darkness and uncertainty. Praise God!

"Though the mountains be shaken, and the hills be removed, yet My Unfailing Love for you will not be shaken nor My Covenant of Peace be removed," says the Lord, Who has Compassion on you." Isaiah 54:10

The Barn - Move In

August of 1989 was the month we were to move into the barn. We had lived in this lovely Brookshire home for a year and there had been no interested buyers during that entire time. I had been faithful to my commitment to make it "California staged" and any showings during that time were ready for inspection. In spite of that preparation, once again God's Kind and Loving Hand had been providing for us during this transition. For the first time since Brookshires put it on the market, a buyer made an acceptable offer. A contract was written and we were moving out just days before it closed! The Lord had given us that beautiful place Perfectly Timed for our need! Once again the Lord revealed His Loving Presence!

Now our apartment over the barn was ready for us! It was a warm August day and there was an excitement as we moved in. The new pine on the floors and woodwork around the windows and doors emitted a fresh, sweet aroma of pine and the golden glow from the afternoon sun coming through the windows captured a delightful entrance. From the window we could see a grove of cottonwood trees, separated by the driveway, lining what was to become the entrance to the pastor's retreat. Also, from here, we could witness the construction progress of the pastor's retreat.

We had called Pastor Kaningater, from Conference Baptist to come and dedicate the property to the Lord and His work. Jim and I were looking forward to living there and being a part of what the Lord was going to do. We wanted the Lord to be the center of everything that took place on this land!

All of this was perfect. But not long after we moved in, our enthusiasm was overshadowed. It was here that we received news that my daddy (83 years old) had passed away. He had been diagnosed with bone cancer the previous year and had had a long and painful battle. He never complained. We knew the time for his homegoing was imminent. My precious father had supported and loved my mother and me all his life. He was faithful, honest, and true. My kind and loving mother had been caring for him in their condo home in Evergreen. They were a couple that lived before us a life of true devotion to one another. They were a week short of being married 57 years. What a blessing the Lord had given Jim, our children and me in having such faithful and God-fearing parents. Daddy will be missed terribly, but I believe that he is very much alive, and I will see him again and we will praise our Precious Savior and King, together forever! Our Lord Jesus said, "I am the Resurrection and the Life. He that believes in Me, though he be dead, yet shall he live and he that lives and believes in Me, shall never die." John 11:25

I believe God's Word with all my heart!

Dark And Deadly Days

Moving into the barn also brought another heavy load that dampened our enthusiasm. During the time of my father's illness, before he passed away, I had noticed a lump on my breast that had been there for some time, but I dismissed it, knowing that I had many benign fibroid cysts. When they were brought to our Dr. Harvey's attention in the past, he said that it was difficult to determine if any were cancerous, even with an x-ray. So I tended to be casual about them, knowing that there was nothing I could do. Also, our attention was on Daddy. He was the one who had cancer! He was the one who was fighting and struggling. He was the one who needed our love, care and attention.

However, soon after my father passed away, I began to see that I had been neglecting the warning signs. I think that I had been in denial. I wasn't the one with cancer, I thought. Daddy was. However, the symptoms were undeniable, and they were getting more and more obvious. I needed to let the doctor check what was happening. After Dr. Harvey examined me, he sent me to a surgeon. The surgeon was 99.9% sure that it was cancer just by looking at it. Dr. Harvey immediately connected me to an oncologist, Dr. Fink. Within the week I was on the operating table having a mastectomy for breast cancer! Expecting the cancer to have spread throughout my body, they also removed all the lymph glands in my left arm. I would need 6 months of chemotherapy and 6 weeks of radiation. The doctors never gave me any hope. They never said that any of this would cure me of this dreaded, deadly disease. I had been carrying it in my body entirely too long. One doctor said that I should have had the surgery long ago! The only hope I heard the oncologist give was when he stated that if I could remain cancer free for five years, then he could be sure that they had gotten it.

October 11, 1990 was when this news hit me like a bomb! My daddy had passed away one year before, almost to the day, of my diagnosis on October 4, 1989. My mother had been a widow for one year. How would she take this? Kevin was living with her while he was working on his Emergency Medical Certificate. Kim was at Wheaton College, finishing her Senior year. Jim was working in real estate and I was teaching school at Marshdale Elementary. We had been living in the apartment over the barn for one year.

When I came home from the doctor's office we had to bear the reality of this dreaded news. Fear, confusion, and panic overtook me. Breast cancer? Surgery? Mastectomy? Six months of chemotherapy? Six weeks of radiation? All of this seemed unattainable to me. I couldn't imagine anticipating tomorrow, much less six months! How did my father carry this with such strength for so long? In the last several years three dear, precious sisters in the Lord in our church body passed away from breast cancer. One was younger than I, and one was the mother of four, for whom we all called upon the Lord to heal. As I lay on my bed trying to go to sleep, all these fears kept whirling through my mind, especially concerning the pastor's retreat. Where was my faith now??

I pondered, "Would the Lord lead us this far and answer my prayers with such detail and accuracy, if He were going to call me home before it bore any fruit?" I paused several minutes thinking about this. "Yes", I thought. He is Sovereign, and His Plans will not be thwarted, whatever they are. I must not lean to my own understanding. Maybe He had someone else in mind to carry on this ministry. His plans are always Good because He is Good. "For My Thoughts are not your thoughts, neither are your ways My Ways, declares the Lord. As the heavens are higher than the earth so are My Ways higher than your ways, and My Thoughts than your thoughts." Isaiah 55:8-9

The next morning, I awakened and saw my Bible on the nightstand. Still thinking about my circumstance, I reached for it and opened it randomly. And the very first words I saw were, "Listen to me!" I took these words as a command! They seemed to shout at me and I wanted to hear what the Lord had to say.

"LISTEN TO ME, YOU WHOM I HAVE UPHELD SINCE YOU WERE CONCEIVED AND HAVE CARRIED SINCE YOUR BIRTH! EVEN TO YOUR OLD AGE AND GRAY HAIRS I AM HE WHO WILL SUSTAIN YOU. I WILL SUSTAIN YOU AND I WILL CARRY YOU; I WILL SUSTAIN YOU AND I WILL RESCUE YOU!" Isaiah 46:3-4

Even though the Lord was saying this to Israel, He was also speaking these same words to me. They were timed right with the concern of my heart. The Lord would rescue me. He had upheld me since I was conceived, and He has carried me since my birth, and He has sustained me, and He will sustain me until I am an old woman with gray hair! I understood this to mean that the Lord will rescue me from the death that cancer could inflict. I wrote in the margin of my Bible the date, October 11, 1990.

"Oh Lord, Thank You for encouraging me with this passage. If I have misunderstood, however, I still believe that You are Wise beyond all Comprehension and I will put my hope in You for the outcome, no matter what! Your Will be done."

I took a sick leave from my teaching position at Marshdale, during the time when the chemo treatments were building in intensity. Then I returned to my duties in January of 1991. During all this time, the parents and children from my class were wonderful. I could expect a new encouraging card every time my next treatment was due. Our church also supported me with much love and concern and many prayers. One Sunday, while I was sitting quietly in a pew after I had been first diagnosed, a woman sat down next to me. The service was about to begin. She never even looked at me and I had never seen her before but suddenly, still not looking at me, in a quiet, clear voice she said to me, "You are going to get well." Did I really hear these words? I wasn't bold enough to ask her to confirm what I thought she said. I didn't even know her. Nothing more was said. She got away quickly, and I never saw her again, but I get "the chills" even now as I remember this.

Because I was employed with Jefferson County Public Schools, I had excellent insurance and my care (even though it was thousands of dollars) was completely covered—every penny.

"Thank You, Lord! Praise You for all Your Care!"

"Cast your cares on the Lord and He will sustain you; He will never let the righteous fall." Psalm 55:22

We're Seeing Spots!

Christmas of 1990 was just around the corner and Jim was hoping to be moved into the Pastor's Retreat by then. I was staying with my mother during my treatment and Jim was working on getting the house ready to move in. He was having the carpet laid the day before Christmas Eve. But when the carpet layers unrolled it, the white carpet was covered with gray spots! Jim was so disappointed, knowing that we could not order in time for our move-in day and be ready to celebrate Christmas, too. He called me on the phone sounding so forlorn and defeated. "I can't do it." he said. "The carpet is holding everything up."

Later, when Jim could talk to the manager and explain the situation concerning my condition, the carpet company reassured Jim that they would replace the spotted carpet with one of finer quality, and have it laid in time for Christmas, free of charge! That was such a blessing for Jim! He wanted me to have a beautiful Christmas in our new, completed home. I know that he thought it might be my last.

Christmas came, and everything was in place...even the furniture! There was nothing in the drawers or cabinets, but everything looked ready to live in. Jim had purchased platters of food from Costco and had invited many people from church and we celebrated with joyous Christmas Carols and praise. With the crackling of the fire in the large fireplace it was a wonderful evening of warmth and love. "Thank You again, Lord, for friends and family and a wonderful, caring husband."

My cancer treatments were completed in June of 1991. It seemed like an eternity at the time. And then it would be five years before we would know if all of this was successful. Would the Lord rescue me and sustain me even to my old age and gray hair as he spoke to me that morning when I was diagnosed? I repeated the words.

"Listen to Me you whom I have upheld since you were conceived and have carried since your birth. Even to your old age and gray hairs I Am He, I Am He Who will sustain you. I have made you and I will carry you; I will sustain you and I will rescue you." Isaiah 46:3-4 I so wanted to believe that!

Jim would go with me, to receive my treatments. He would always hold my hand during the entire treatment. On one occasion I was crying and having a pity party. Poor me! Jim very quietly and kindly said, "You better pray about your attitude." I realized that he was right! God was so Good to me in so many ways. If He saw fit to put this in my life, I ought to Rejoice in His Wisdom to do so. If He takes me home to be with Him, so be it.

Until then, He tells us in James 1:2-3, that we are to "Consider it all Joy, my brethren, when you go through various trials knowing that the testing of your faith produces endurance and let endurance have its perfect result that you may be perfect and lacking nothing." At that point, I asked the Lord to give me Joy in going through this and see it from His perspective. He granted my prayer. People often remarked, "Why are you so happy when you have cancer?"

"You Hear, O Lord, the desire of the Afflicted; You Encourage them, and You Listen to their cry in order that man, who is of the Earth, may terrify no more." Psalm 10:17, 18

Dean And Karen

Horses and saddles, bridles and lead ropes, wranglers and cowboys! When I was a little girl living in Detroit, Michigan, I loved horses! I would cut out pictures of horses. I would draw horses. I would collect little statues of horses. I even made a stick horse out of the wooden stick that was used in the window shade to steady it. The cardboard head of the horse was taken from the packaging of my father's professionally laundered shirts. I would carefully draw its eyes, mouth and mane. After cutting it out, I would tape it to the end of the stick, making a stick horse! Then I would ride it proudly all over the sidewalks in my Detroit neighborhood. I even named my bike "Thunder", and I didn't think of it as a bicycle. It was my horse! I would follow the milk wagon down the street just to watch the horse with its feed bag over his muzzle. The large horse would slowly and powerfully pull the milk wagon to each curbside where the milk man would jump out and deliver the milk. I always wanted a horse and I prayed that someday I would have either a horse or a dog. Sometimes I would look in the back of a magazine and see advertisements for guest ranches or dude ranches and thought how nice it would be to visit a ranch like that. There would be horses, horses, horses!

Now, as I gazed through the window of this lovely new home, I recalled the days of long ago when I was just a little girl, living in the city of Detroit and horses were my obsession. Today, I looked off in the distance, at the neighbors next door and realized all those prayers that I prayed in childlike faith, were heard by a Kind and Loving God, my "Abba Father!" We were now living next door to a thriving guest ranch called, "The North Fork Guest Ranch." Dean and Karen May were the owners.

For our 27th wedding anniversary, Jim had some frequent flier miles to go anywhere in the world. He asked me where I would like to go for our anniversary. Immediately I answered, "to the Guest Ranch next door!" Now you must understand this was a Five-Star, very expensive operation, and it provided in one week everything from trail rides to skeet shooting, to fly fishing, to swimming, to river rafting the Colorado River, to square dancing and eating fancy home-cooked gourmet meals! We gave the frequent flier miles to Kim and Kevin and we did all the ranch had to offer. We truly had a wonderful time. We were prepared to pay just like everyone else, but they would have none of that. Dean and Karen proved, through the many years, to be among the most generous and gracious people we have ever known. We grew to love them.

We had gladly given Dean permission to take their horse rides across our bridge to enter the National Forest, so we periodically could watch the horses and riders cross over the bridge

and pass through. It was such a pleasant sight. Because of the lush growth in our meadow, we also gave permission for them to graze our 10 acres on the other side of our property. Seeing their horses grazing against a blue sky and a carpet of green, lined with white plank fence is enchanting. Then I recalled my request of God, as a little child, asking for a horse or a dog, and how nice it would be to visit a guest ranch. In my recollection of events in my life, beginning at age eight, I have had five dogs and eight horses throughout my lifetime. There was never a time that I didn't have one or the other! The Lord granted me the pleasure of not only visiting a guest ranch, but also living next door to one!

"Lord, You continue to amaze me! When I gave my life to You at the young age of 13 years old in the quiet of my bedroom, expressing fear in what You might ask me to do, I never dreamed that Your plans for me would be so Gracious, so Kind. You overwhelm me with Your Goodness! I'm so undeserving! Please let me live in a way that pleases You in response to Your incredible Goodness! I'm reminded of the verse in Psalm 37:4 "Delight yourself in the Lord and He will give you the desires of your heart." You have repeatedly given me the desires of my heart!

When I was praying in California for the pastor's retreat and understanding that it would probably be in a rural area, I believed that we would need neighbors who would be a good deal younger and would be helpful towards us as we aged. Realizing this, I asked that the Lord if He saw fit, to please provide. There they were! Dean and Karen May were there the whole time we were contemplating the purchase of the David Ray property. It didn't dawn on me that they were an answer to that request. We were 25 years older than they, and they felt that we were old then! We didn't feel older, at all. We were looking to what the Lord had for us in this new chapter of our lives, cancer and all. I feel certain that they really felt like we were heading for the grave when I was diagnosed with cancer. So, from the start of our relationship as their neighbors, they had a tenderness and a sense of compassion for us.

Where Jim had temporarily put up wire fencing to keep our horses in, we thought it would be prettier, with the style of our home, to put up white plank, Blue Grass Kentucky fencing. So Jim began to dig the post holes. This would be a very big task, seeing that it was like the river, half a mile of it. Jim said that he liked the work and he would chip away at the task. Dean, seeing what Jim was undertaking, intervened saying, "I can have my wranglers dig those post holes and put those fences up in their down time." And they did! It was beautiful. They worked all summer, during their down time and had the property lined with a lovely white plank fence. Jim painted it, which was task enough!

During the snowy months our God sent these precious neighbors to plow snow off of our long winding driveway, all the way to our door! This is the way Dean and Karen responded to us throughout our almost 30 years together as neighbors. We reciprocated with helps to them also, but we never took care of them like they did us. All in all, we became very good neighbors to one another.

Countless times Dean and Karen invited us down to their daily dinners. We even on several occasions brought an additional guest with us. These dinners featured wild game, such as buffalo and rainbow trout cooked to perfection!

During the summer months their outdoor pool was opened to us anytime, without even asking! We always asked anyway. We didn't want to wear out a good thing or behave as if it was ours. This was a highlight of our grandchildren's visits! They thoroughly enjoyed this as well as the petting zoo and a homemade cookie from Karen on each of their visits.

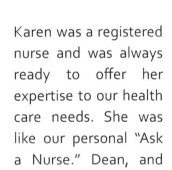

Karen was a registered nurse and was always ready to offer her expertise to our health care needs. She was like our personal "Ask a Nurse." Dean, and now his lovely daughter and her husband, accommodated our need for hay and grain to be delivered to feed our horses. They even saved us garbage pick-up cost by letting us use their dumpster! All these things have been going on for the 26 years we lived in Shawnee. I believe that Dean and Karen were the answer to my prayer concerning the help we would need living in this beautiful place.

"Thank You, again Lord! I am humbled again by Your responses to my prayers. Thank You for Dean and Karen's willingness to be so kind and gracious. Lord, I can't help but ponder the complexity of the work You do to put all these details together! You are Awesome!"
"The Lord Watches over all who love Him." Psalm 145:20

The Carriage House

When Jim and I lived in the barn while our house was being completed we would often walk over to see the progress of the pastor's retreat. Every time we completed our tour, we would be anxious to return to our little cabin. It really seemed like home. I had decorated it with antiques and a cowboy/western theme, with rich colors of amber, forest green and burgundy. Everything came together with the golden pine floors and wood work trim and it gave a cozy, inviting bid to come and relax.

I thought of all the things I had prayed and now, in comparison I could see how pastors and their families would enjoy the privacy of this little cabin more than a confined room with white carpet! The flowery room upstairs in our home with the hot tub for two was inviting. But the cabin provided flexibility for meals and with the fully equipped kitchen and ability to cook, it really was a place which could become a home away from home. It could conform to their special needs and accommodate the pastors with a more relaxed and private place.

"But Lord," I queried. "What will we do with our big, fancy bedroom upstairs?" He assured me that it would be used for His purposes. He had paid for it and directed the construction of it also. It was His and for His use.

 This little cabin became a special place nestled in the magnificent foothills of the great Colorado Rocky Mountains. It was perfect! The beauty of this plan for a cabin was a masterpiece not thought of by me, and was painted stroke by stroke by the Hand of God. It evolved in our minds through the Lord's Revelation. He knew all along what He wanted. At this point, I believed many servants of the Lord would be encouraged, restored and refreshed in such a place.

There were expenses in operating the cabin. The property taxes went up, there were bills for heat and electricity. So I again asked the Lord for the provision to support such a ministry without asking the pastors for anything...not even a "love offering." I knew for sure that the Lord would provide, but at this point, there had been no answer. One day Karen May came over to ask a favor of us. She had seen the cabin and its "charm." I knew that their guest ranch was successful and sometimes they had too many calls for reservations.

She asked, "Would you be interested in renting your guest house to us for the summer?" I didn't even need to think about it! I knew that this was our answer! The Lord was once again using Karen and Dean to fulfill another answer to my prayer. Because their ranch was a high-end guest ranch, they attracted a high-end clientele, and they were willing to pay us a generous amount. The sum would be more

than if we would have rented it to a stranger a whole year.

Because they needed a way to identify the cabin, it needed a name. Jim suggested the Carriage House, so that became its name. The amount we received was exactly the amount necessary to cover the expenses of the Carriage House!

"We marvel at You, Oh Lord. Your Presence is involved in everything in our lives!"

"Now to Him Who is able to do Immeasurably more than all we ask or Imagine, according to His Power that is at work within us, to Him be Glory in the church and in Christ Jesus throughout all Generations, Forever and Ever! Amen." Ephesians 3:20,21

James Dobson! Really?

With everything completed, Jim suggested we visit Colorado Springs, making an appointment with Focus on the Family. Maybe we could participate with them in offering the Carriage House as a respite to pastors who would benefit from such a place. Their ministry called, "Under His Wings" which was overseen by H. B. London, ministered to pastors and their families and was well established. Jim thought they would be a good contact to help us get started. We would tell them of our desire and what has been provided to fulfill that desire. We could take pictures of The Carriage House and the area and ask if they would be willing to direct pastors, with whom it would be appropriate, to our facility. This we did.

My dear mother was so happy and excited that we were going to see James Dobson! I told her we were not going to see James Dobson. James Dobson was too busy to see us, and our appointment was with Roger Charmin. Even though I told her this, she would continue to refer to our trip to Colorado Springs as, "going to see James Dobson."

On the day of our appointment Jim and I gathered up all our pictures, put them in a little photo album and headed for Colorado Springs. When we arrived, we were asked to wait in the entry until called. There was a lot of activity in this area. Tripods were being set up. Lights were put in place and suddenly James Dobson appeared! He was going to make a TV shoot. Jim looked at me and I looked at him. Did my mother know something we didn't know?

A gentleman saw us sitting there and came over and introduced himself and asked us about the nature of our visit. We told him that we had an appointment with Roger Charmin to speak to him about our Carriage House. We showed him our pictures and told him what we had in mind. At this point, he asked us if we would like to speak to Dr. Dobson! "Of course, we would!" We exclaimed together! This gentleman left us for a moment then came back with Dr. Dobson, who had a big wonderful smile and wanted to hear all about what we desired to do. We had a delightful conversation and he encouraged us. He was glad that the Lord had moved us to think about such a ministry. On the ride home, Jim and I had to laugh at my mother's persistence in telling us that we were going to Colorado Springs to see Dr. Dobson. She was absolutely right!

Me, A Bible Study Teacher?

Even though we were only 40 minutes away from Conference Baptist Church, we began to feel the need to attend a church more local. But, while going through the cancer treatments I wasn't motivated to start serving in any capacity except to attend worship services. So until these treatments were completed, we waited before jumping into church membership somewhere else. We attended a community church, Platte Canyon Community Church.

Time passed and I was beginning to approach my fifth year since being diagnosed with cancer. It was 1995. I had been receiving the necessary regular check-ups with Dr. Fink, the oncologist. Jim and I had become good friends with him as Jim would always come with me for my check-ups. When my appointment was made for my annual check-up, I felt it was quite routine and I really didn't think too much about it until after Dr. Fink completed the check-up and stated, "Sharon, you are completely free from cancer! You are no more likely to have cancer return than any other person who has never had cancer. We got it all!" Those words were like a jolt of super energy that raced through my body like lightning! I felt so free! I didn't realize that carrying the thought of that cancer being in my body had such a weight on me! I had a new perspective on life!

We had grown very fond of the people at Platte Canyon Community Church and so we attended three more years. This is where I was introduced to "Precepts Bible Study" which was an in-depth inductive Bible study by Kay Arthur. Conference Baptist Church had been using this material and praised it, so I was encouraged to see what made it so good.

Sharon Flaningan from Platte Canyon was teaching one of the inductive studies on Philippians, so I decided to join her class. I loved it! When I would go through the lessons, I took up so much paper writing what I was learning, that the workbook wouldn't hold it all. The Observation Worksheets were covered with notes. On one occasion Sharon walked by my desk seeing my open workbook and all that I had written. She exclaimed, "My goodness, you have written so much!" I told her that I was learning so much. She said to me, "Do you see anyone else writing that much?" Then she added, "You should be a teacher!"

Those words rang in my ears and I remembered the time when I was living with Aunt Ree and Uncle Andrew. I was upstairs by myself, in Judy's bedroom, teaching my imaginary students. I was talking out-loud giving instruction with much animation and enthusiasm and I was totally uninhibited, lost in my imaginary world. My voice must have carried down the stairwell. I heard Uncle Andrew, who was reading the Bible in his favorite arm chair say with a voice straining to whisper, as if that would conceal the oddity of what he had heard, "Marie, listen to Sharon upstairs talking to herself." He thought that was rather strange. That didn't offend me at all. Having been an only child, one had to create pleasant characters and situations, and this was one for me.

I remembered the Lord's call on my life when I was 13 years old and I gave my life to the Lord. I thought even then, if He were calling me into full-time ministry, it would be as a Christian Education Director.

I remembered the first time I had heard an expository presentation of the Scriptures. We had begun to attend Canoga Park Baptist Church in California. The teacher's name was Eddie Woo. He was the adult Sunday School teacher and his class was packed! Obviously, he had the gift of teaching and his attention to handling the Word accurately was clear. Upon hearing him, a strong wave of longing filled me. I said in my heart, "I would so love to present the Word of God with such clarity and power."

I remember even in public school the pleasure I had in teaching for 13 years. In church, I also had taught Sunday School, directed Vacation Bible School, Junior Church and puppet ministries. All these areas of service are under the heading of Christian Education, even though I did not have a degree in Christian Education. The Lord, in His foreknowledge, called me to these things when I was 13 years old. He created good works for me to walk in...degree or not!

Ephesians 2:10 "For we are His Workmanship, Created in Christ Jesus for Good Works, which God Prepared Beforehand so that we would walk in them."

Now here was Sharon Flanigan, telling me that I should be a teacher of Precept Bible Study! This caught my attention and really what I had been looking for ever since my cousin, Jo Florence, modeled this for me each night before she went to bed—attention to God's Word. Because I had witnessed Eddie Woo's class, so fed with the richness of the Scripture, I hungered after it more. This inductive study, a method used in seminaries, would help me handle the Word accurately. Upon getting further information, I learned that a training class was required before one could teach the Precept Upon Precept Inductive Study. I gladly took the class and I was excited to have a group of women who were interested in an in-depth Bible study. The Women's Bible Study called "Precept upon Precept" by Kay Arthur was begun!

Crow Hill Bible Church

For some time, Jim and I had been watching a small church in our community called Crow Hill Bible Church - just 15 minutes from our house. It was a small sister church that was begun with the help of our former church in Evergreen, Conference Baptist. It had an attendance of about 90 people. We felt that the Lord was leading us to serve there. In my enthusiasm to get started there, I encouraged two whole car loads of people from our congregation to be trained to teach Precepts! This was 1998. I was thrilled with all the opportunities and I felt the Lord giving me not only the desire to get involved but also the enablement. I felt a motivation that I had never felt before. It was happy and joyful, energetic and full of expectancy, and anticipation for the future.

One beautiful morning I went for a walk down our driveway. "You spared me, Lord!" I declared. The birds were singing. The sun was warm and bright. I was free from cancer and I was very grateful! At this point, I asked the Lord what He wanted me to do with the time He had given me. Later in my quiet time, the Lord gave me, once again the passage in Psalm 37:3-7: "Trust in the Lord and do good; dwell in the land and enjoy safe pasture. Delight yourself in the Lord and He will give you the desires of your heart. Commit your way to the Lord; trust in Him and He will do this. He will make your righteousness shine like the dawn and the justice of your cause like the noonday sun. Be still before the Lord, wait patiently for Him..."

In the following years, I witnessed the Lord giving me many opportunities to "do good" and dwell in the peaceful and safe pasture He had provided. The Lord was Delightful! And to continue to wait on Him for His direction continued to be our habit as Jim and I served in our beloved church, Crow Hill Bible. We continued to exercise our spiritual gifts within the body of believers and truly loved the people with whom we served...and since contact with Focus on the Family, and Under His Wings Ministry, we have had and are still having wonderful experiences hosting pastors and their families.

Under His Wings

"You, Oh Lord, are giving me the joy of the ministry for which I prayed for so many years! Praise your name, Lord." The ministry was begun. Since we asked to be included in the *Under His Wings* ministry with Focus on the Family, pastors were calling from all over the United States. We even had missionaries. We were overjoyed!

The display of the Lord's Presence as He Miraculously moved His Hand was always Timed Perfectly! I stood in awe every time I thought back to those early days of praying. The waiting on His answers and the speed and timing in which He answered, when His timing was in place, was spectacular! God's Presence was so obvious in His answers. No one could have done the things that took place except the Hand of the Loving, Powerful, One and Only Creator — God! All of this was exceeding, abundantly beyond more than I could ask or think! My faith in my Precious Lord and Savior will never be shaken. The display of His reality in my life has been consistent for my entire life and continues, even as I write this.

I flashed back to the time in California when our children were little, and I prayed that after they were raised I would have the privilege to serve pastors in a peaceful, beautiful place. I remembered the verses that inspired me.

"It was for the sake of the name that they went out, receiving no help from the pagans. We ought therefore to show hospitality to such men so that we may work together for the truth." 3 John 1:7-8

"Send them on their way in a manner worthy of God." 3 John 1:16

"I waited patiently for the Lord; He turned to me and heard my cry. He set my feet on a rock and gave me a firm place to stand. He put a new song in my mouth, a hymn of praise to our God. Many will see and fear and put their trust in the Lord." Psalm 40:11, 12

God's beautiful place for pastors was begun and it was a blessing to see. This was 1995. I had been praying since 1975, 20 years! God's Perfect Timing!

North Fork River

Isaiah 55:12 declares "You will ago out in joy and be led forth in peace; the mountains and hills will burst into song before you, and all the trees of the field will clap their hands!"

I stood down by the edge of the river, among the mountains and hills and all the trees of the field. Many were gathered from our church to witness the testimonies of those desiring to follow Christ in baptism. I thought about Jesus, being baptized in the chilly Jordan River and here we were witnessing the Lord's plan for this river. My heart was racing in the fact that the Lord was using this lovely, chilly mountain river for such a holy privilege. I had never thought of such a thing when David Ray first introduced us to the property. The Lord surprised me with this!

"Thank You, Lord for giving us so much to be used for Your Glory."

My attention turned to all the testimonies and I was touched listening to each precious one. Tears filled my eyes. What an elation I felt as each one professed their faith, coming from the old life and going to the new; now raised up through the waters of baptism, picturing newness of life! At that point, as each person was raised up, the water would splash and roar, their bodies resisting the weight of the water. Everyone would clap and cheer and praise the Lord with "Hallelujahs!" When I remember Isaiah 55:12, I can almost hear the mountains and hills bursting into song at such a moment, and all the trees of the field clapping their hands!

There is great joy that comes from the testimony of a heart that is fully surrendered to the Lord and pictured in the waters of baptism; dying to self and raised to newness of life! Things inanimate, the mountains, the hills, the trees of the field responding to one who will go out in joy, led forth in peace. What a blessing to have witnessed over 100 such, in this beautiful river! "Thank You, Lord!"

The Guest Room

The room is all vacuumed and dusted. The tile in the private bathroom sparkles. The pillows are fluffed, and Jim's grandmother's hand crocheted pillow cases are ready for gracing the buoyant feather bed. Her handmade quilt is laid across the back of a small bedroom chair and the vivid colors in the quilt visually set a country garden mood, repeating the Victorian floral in the wallpaper. There is a lovely stained-glass window on the door that leads out to the small balcony. The room is stately looking, with the high ceiling and dramatic views of the river below, and yet very comfortable and inviting.

For our overnighters, the windows are ready to be opened for the sound of the river's lullaby and the cool mountain night air to be invited in. This special room awaits the next guests who can be embraced with this sweet repose. There is something wonderful about sleeping under the stars of the Colorado sky and listening to the gentle hum of the flowing river.

This was the room that was built for the pastors and their wives and even though some have used it, the Lord has had other plans. Because we have had this extra guest room, there have been many dear friends and many in our precious, loving family who have blessed us with their visits. Each has been special, and it has been a joy to share with all who have come. We look forward to the Lord continuing to bring us this opportunity.

"It's been such a blessing Lord. Thank You for all of Your Unexpected Plans!"

How Astonishing Are Your Ways

Stirring eggs over an open fire, fresh trout sizzling in butter and lemon, yeast rolls with a softness only homemade in Karen's oven can bake, smells of sausage and bacon. These were the sights and smells of the Champagne Brunch that the North Fork Guest Ranch offered to their guests every Tuesday. It was a trail ride on horseback to the spot just perfect for such a special event. The views were spectacular, overlooking the immensity of the 13,000 acres of Pike National Forest in Shawnee, Colorado.

There was always something to see, so we were anxious to accept the invitation to visit the other guest ranch in the area called, "Tumbling River." One of Dean's wranglers told us to hop in his truck; it wasn't very far up the road. We hopped in and drove about 15 minutes. The scenery was lovely with all the evergreens lining the road on each side. Suddenly, as I saw a break in the trees there was a beautiful waterfall. It was clear and clean, sparkling as the droplets caught the sun. The water was racing down the mountain side, splashing with white caps and a loud roar. The evergreens were lining each side of it. "Wow!" I exclaimed with astonished surprise. "That is a beautiful waterfall!" "Oh, yes," said the wrangler. "That watefall was used by Coors Beer to advertise their beer. It's pictured on the back of magazines." I was stunned! What was he saying? The image of that waterfall advertising Coors Beer on the back of a magazine was brought to my mind! There it was on our night stand by our bed, used by God to direct us to this beautiful place, just 15 minutes from here! Upon seeing this waterfall on the back of that magazine, I can still hear my voice shouting excitedly these words, "a place *just like that*, Lord, ***Just Like That!***"

"Oh Lord, how faithful You are and how astonishing are Your ways! You faithfully led us to a place where there are things, '***Just Like That***' and it was in Your Perfect Timing!"

Responses Over The Years

I am now 75 years old. Jim is 78. The Carriage House has been refreshing pastors now for 22 years and it has been our blessing! I have always been amazed at how people have responded to their visits. I know that the reason this little cabin does its job, is because all of it has been God's work and provision to accomplish. I have been so privileged to have witnessed the Hand of God move through the years! We have had literally hundreds and hundreds of precious servants of the Lord use this respite these 22 years and we are still taking reservations! We also have hundreds and hundreds of thank you notes expressing gratitude for the opportunity to rest in this beautiful place. Here are some excerpts from the hundreds of responses that were written in the guest books:

"Thank you for the respite, the beauty and the quiet. Thank you for pouring out the blessings God has given. I am so blessed, and I thank God for you!" Hosea 6:1-3

"Grateful! Grateful to God and grateful to you for sharing your place with me again; this is my fifth visit" II Corinthians 11-12 "Your gift overflowing in thanksgiving to God." "Utterly grateful!"

"We thank God every time we remember you," ...and the blessings of His loving kindness when we come here for a retreat and rest. Love and prayers and many thanks."

"Thank you so much for your generosity in allowing us to stay at the Carriage House. We have enjoyed our time away. We were here 16 years ago with all 4 of our sons. It was great to come back again! This time just the two of us."

"Thank you so much for providing this wonderful place to stay. We enjoyed it so much. The views are incredible! We needed a break, and this was the best! May God richly bless you!"

"Dear Jim and Sharon, thank you so much for this time of being able to enjoy God's beautiful countryside by staying in your Carriage House. You have been a tremendous blessing to us! We had a wonderful time and enjoyed our time as a family. Thank you for making us feel privileged to be a pastor and family! Love you!"

"Thank you for opening your Carriage House to us in our time of need. It was a harbor in the storm in more ways than one! A place for us while we planned and grieved with our son during the death of Harry.

A place to be sorrowful, but a place of peace! The peace of God which passes all understanding shall keep your hearts and minds through Christ Jesus. You blessed us."

"Thank you for a wonderful stay! It was our first time here, and we loved it! Thank you for understanding the life of ministry and for providing a place of rest for our family. We pray that God continues to bless you and your family for your kindness and generosity! Blessings."

"Thanks so much for another wonderful stay in the Carriage House! And for reaching out to us especially to offer us this place when someone else canceled. God timed that beautifully for us in terms of giving us a time of repose before the holidays and in terms of beautiful hiking weather! Thank you for continually making yourselves available to Him and to us!"

"Another great stay! Thanks for the blessing! It always feels like home here. I love you both dearly!"

"Thank you for this restful place. This was our 40th Anniversary. Beautiful stay, dear friends!"

"What a delight to return to your neck of the woods! Thank you for your continued ministry in our lives. Through you, God has provided the perfect haven for refueling and reconnecting and a treasury of priceless memories. May our Lord bless you abundantly! Thank you for sharing yourselves with us."

"You're the best, Jim and Sharon! Thank you, a million times, over! Only God can bless you enough for your great labor of love! We love you bunches!"

"Jim and Sharon, Thank you so much for your generous act of hospitality. Each one of us enjoyed our time so much and Brian and I sincerely appreciate the opportunity to enjoy God's beautiful creation here. A sincere thank you. You make us feel privileged to be a pastor's family! Love you!"

"Thanks again for allowing us to come and be refreshed spirit, soul, and body! The Spirit of the Lord's rest can be felt the moment we arrive here. I remember how the Lord told His disciples to, 'come and rest for a while.' This is the place that the Lord brings His servants when He tells us today to come and rest for a while. May God's extravagant blessings be upon you and your entire family."

"We loved being here and doing so many things we enjoy... fishing, hiking, jigsaw puzzles, relaxing, traveling on the Tarryall Heritage Tour, sleeping, visiting parks like Staunton and Pine Valley, picnicking, making s'mores, catching up on reading, exploring, eating out, having cozy fires, being outside in beautiful weather, and marveling at the lovely fall foliage. Thank you for making this restful time possible for us."

To My Children

Of all the prayers I have ever prayed and for all the things I have ever longed, none have been more urgent and fervent in my life than the prayers I have uttered for my precious children.

This prayer, on the next page, was taken from Ephesians 1:16. I copied it before you who are now my grandchildren were even born — but my longing for each of you, beginning with Kim and Kevin has always been within me. I pray that each of you: Kim, Neil, Kevin, Shannon, Rachel, Cara, Lauren, Chad, Moses, Sereyana, and Elijah will come before the Lord with this Scripture and know that I desire every Word of it for each of you.

This little book was written with you in mind. I wanted to share with you the wonder and splendor of trusting a Living and Loving Heavenly Father Who is closer to each of us than breath itself — and Who created us to know Him and give Him Glory for how wonderful He is! We were created for that very purpose! As Ephesians declares, "that your heart will be flooded with light so that you can see something of the future He has called you to share!...and you will begin to understand how incredibly Great His Power is to help those who believe Him."

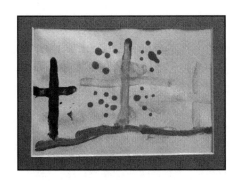

To My Children

I have never stopped thanking God for you. I pray for you constantly, asking God, the glorious Father of our Lord Jesus Christ, to give you wisdom to see clearly and really understand who Christ is and all that he has done for you. I pray that your hearts will be flooded with light so that you can see something of the future he has called you to share. I want you to realize that God has been made rich because we who are Christ's have been given to him! I pray that you will begin to understand how incredibly great his power is to help those who believe him.

Ephesians 1:16

Jim and Sharon with Kim and Kevin

Kevin and Shannon

Kim and Neil

Kim, Sereyana, Moses, Neil, and Elijah

Moses, Elijah, and Sereyana

Kevin, Lauren, Cara, Shannon, Chad, and Rachel

Rachel, Chad, Cara, and Lauren

Promises Fulfilled

My book was finished! I was looking forward to turning it over to Amy Allen, a bubbly sweet graphic design artist to whom I was led by the Lord, through the Carriage House. She and her family had been visiting the Carriage house with some precious missionaries from "Jews for Jesus." I was so thrilled that she was going to be involved with the cover and interior design! On this particular morning when Amy was coming to help me, she was rather excited and wanted to share with me why. "Did you notice today's date?" she said enthusiastically. She began to tell me how she had been reading her daily devotion in "Our Daily Bread" for October 11, 2018...today's date. She said, "That was exactly the same date you recorded in the margin of your Bible 28 years ago, when you had been diagnosed with cancer the day before!" Yes! I recorded that date, October 11, 1990, because that was when the Lord had given me the passage in Isaiah 46:3-4 that explained how the Lord had upheld me, and would rescue me, and sustain me to my old age and gray hairs! *"Listen to Me, you whom I have upheld since you were conceived, and have carried since your birth. Even to your old age and gray hairs. I am He, I am He Who will sustain you. I have made you and I will carry you; I will sustain you and will rescue you."* Obviously, God was drawing our attention to that particular date.

What does this tell us about God? God was true to His Word! At the time, 28 years ago, I wanted to believe what the Lord was telling me through that passage so miraculously and timely revealed, but now I SEE through the passing of all these years how Faithful the Lord was in fulfilling what He told me on that date! He DID rescue me from that deadly disease, cancer! He HAS sustained me! This book would not have been complete unless I would proclaim the Grace and Love in which God poured into His Words to sustain me. Just as all this

Our Daily Bread

SEPTEMBER • OCTOBER • NOVEMBER 2018

Surely your goodness and love will follow me all the days of my life, and I will dwell in the house of the LORD forever.

PSALM 23:6

★ For Sharon

THURSDAY • OCTOBER 11

THE BIBLE in ONE YEAR
ISAIAH 37–38 and COLOSSIANS 3

Stories of Jesus

As a girl I loved to visit my small local library. One day, looking at the bookshelves holding the young adult section, I reasoned I could probably read every book. In my enthusiasm I forgot one important fact—new books were regularly added to the shelves. Although I gave it a valiant effort, there were simply too many books.

New books continue to fill more and more bookshelves. The apostle John likely would be amazed with the availability of books today since his five New Testament books, the Gospel of John; 1, 2, and 3 John; and Revelation, were handwritten on parchment scrolls.

TODAY'S READING
1 Jn. 1:1–4; Jn. 21:24–25

Jesus did many other things as well. John 21:25

John wrote those books because he felt compelled by the Holy Spirit to give Christians an eyewitness account of Jesus's life and ministry (1 JOHN 1:1–4). But John's writings contained only a small fraction of all that Jesus did and taught during His ministry. In fact, John said if everything Jesus did were written down "the whole world could not contain the books that would be written" (JOHN 21:25 NLT).

John's claim remains true today. Despite all the books that have been written about Jesus, the libraries of the world still cannot contain every story of His love and grace. We can also celebrate that we have our own personal stories to share and rejoice that we will be proclaiming them forever! (PSALM 89:1).

LISA SAMRA

To write the love of God above would drain the ocean dry.
Nor could the scroll contain the whole, though stretched from sky to sky.
F.M. LEHMAN

Let your life tell the story of Christ's love and grace.

revelation was sinking into my heart, and all I wanted to do was fall on my face with thanksgiving and gratitude, Amy went on with her story. "There's more!" She asked me to read the devotional for that day, October 11, 2018. As I read, once again, the Lord had chosen to make His Presence known! The message from the devotional concerned the apostle John and his desire to share all that Jesus had done, but knew that the whole world could not contain the books that would be written. This sounded like the prologue to my book! The ending of the day's devotional was a plea to celebrate the fact that we, as God's children, have our own personal stories to share and in which we rejoice, and the Lord was giving us His encouragement and affirmation that we will be proclaiming them forever! What a confirmation to receive from the gospel of John in these final words to us. "Lord, Thank You, Thank You! Thank You!!!"

Epilogue

If you are a child of God, you have a testimony concerning your life. It's the work of the Holy Spirit to bring you to the knowledge of your need for the Savior and His work that brings you to becoming a mature Christian. This is the process that the Lord has for you and the fulfillment of His purpose in creating you in the first place!

If you are not a child of God, ask the Lord Jesus to come into your heart and forgive you for your sins; tell Him that you want to surrender your life to Him and follow Him from this day forward. He wants you to know Him and recognize His Presence when He is especially demonstrating His Love. He wants you to thank Him for His answers and acknowledge He is the Lord over all things—even over every minute of your life! He wants you to be a witness of what He has done for you and He wants you to proclaim it. I would encourage you to write it and draw attention to the Miraculous things God has done for you. Recognize that with the Lord is the Fountain of Life and your life is important! In Christ, your life will give God Glory!

I join with the apostle John—there have been many, so many other things that Jesus did in my life that I have not included in this account. The details are so numerous I suppose the heavenly state of eternity will be the only place given enough time to proclaim all the wonders of the Lord's Loving, Miraculous Hand upon each of us during this journey we call, "life." When all is said and done, we will bow down and praise Him forever and ever in gratitude! ...and even that will not be enough praise!

Psalm 40:5 declares, "Many, O Lord my God are the Wonders You have done. Things You planned for us no one can recount to You; were I to speak and tell of them, they would be too many to declare."

I conclude this epilogue with a prayer. "Dear Heavenly Father, You have revealed so many things about Yourself as I have lived these 75 years in the life You have given me. All that You have said about Yourself in Your Word is true! You have demonstrated Your attributes and character in my daily affairs and made me so often know Your Presence. You are Gracious, slow to anger, Compassionate, Merciful, Kind, abounding in Lovingkindness and Truth and always Good. Yet, You do not allow wickedness to go unpunished. You are Pure and Holy and so, "other" than we are. As Psalm 8 declares, "What is man that thou are mindful of him?" Yet Your Love is Tender and Personal, and You are always Mindful of us. Psalm 139:3 reminds me that, "You scrutinize my path! You are intimately acquainted with all of my ways!" "You hear my every prayer and call to You." Psalm 4:3

"I will sing to the Lord all my life; I will sing praise to my God as long as I live." Psalm 104:33, 34

"I want to thank You, Lord for guiding me to write this testimony concerning Your Presence and Reality in my life. It has been a joy and a privilege to recount these evidences of Your Love for me. Truly Goodness and Mercy have followed me all the days of my life! I ask that each person who reads this testimony, will through its pages, accept Your plan for salvation through Jesus as their Lord and Savior! Help them see that only then can they have this wonderful, intimate relationship with You. You gave Your Only Begotten Son so that our sins would not separate us from Your Love and Amazing Mercy! Our sins would not separate us from You, the One and Only Living Creator, God! This witness can begin right now for them Lord, as they surrender their lives to You and accept Your Son as the One Who died in their place for their sins. Please open their eyes Lord, so they too can see that their lives are important to You and that they may proclaim Your Glory, Your Reality, Greatness and Goodness according to their own personal eye witness account! May they join the myriads upon myriads in the chorus of believers who will be praising You Lord, Forever and Ever!"

"My mouth will speak in Praise of the Lord. Let every creature Praise His Holy Name forever and ever." Psalm 145:21

These things I pray in Jesus' Holy Name.

To God Be The Glory!

Made in the USA
Middletown, DE
06 July 2020

12114142R00106